The Dales 30

A Guide to the Mountains of the Dales

by

Jonathan Smith

*"The Dales have a serene beauty
found nowhere else in Britain"*

Published by Where2walk

The Dales 30

First Published 2017
Second Edition Published 2020

ISBN 978-0-9956735-1-9

Front Cover Photo. Buckden Pike looking west

Designed and published by Where2walk

Printed by Briggs Brothers, Cononley BD20 8LG

Contents

Listing

	Page No.	Map Ref	Height (ft)	Height (m)
THE HOWGILLS				
The Calf	14	13	2,218	676
Calders	14	15	2,216	675
Fell Head	18	23	2,099	640
Yarlside	22	24	2,096	639
Randygill Top	22	27	2,047	624
CUMBRIAN PENNINES				
Baugh Fell, Tarn Rigg	30	12	2,224	678
Wild Boar Fell	34	5	2,323	708
Swarth Fell	34	10	2,234	681
High Seat	38	4	2,326	709
Little Fell	38	20	2,188	667
NORTHERN DALES				
Rogan's Seat	46	17	2,205	672
Great Knoutberry Hill	50	16	2,205	672
Great Shunner Fell	54	3	2,349	716
Lovely Seat	54	14	2,214	675
Dodd Fell Hill	58	18	2,192	668
Drumaldrace, Wether Fell	58	28	2,014	614
UPPER WHARFEDALE				
Great Whernside	66	6	2,310	704
Buckden Pike	70	7	2,303	702
Yockenthwaite Moor	74	22	2,110	643
Birks Fell	78	29	2,003	610
WESTERN DALES				
Fountains Fell	86	19	2,192	668
Darnbrook Fell	86	26	2,047	624
Pen-y-Ghent	90	8	2,277	694
Plover Hill	90	11	2,231	680
Ingleborough	94	2	2,375	724
Simon Fell, Ingleborough	94	21	2,129	649
Whernside	98	1	2,415	736
Great Coum	102	9	2,254	687
Gragareth	102	25	2,060	628
Calf Top	106	30	2,000	610

Map

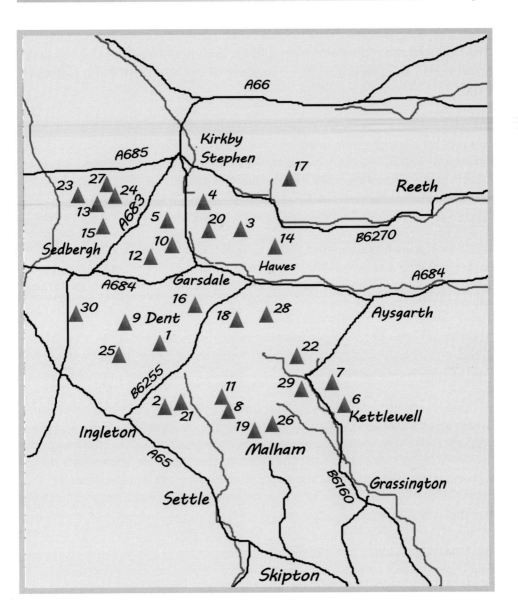

The numbers on the map above relate to the Dales 30 in order of size.
To find them in the book refer to the page opposite under 'Map Ref'.

Introduction to...

The Dales 30 are mountains over 2,000ft (610m) with a 30m (98.4ft) drop on all sides. They sit within the boundary of the Yorkshire Dales National Park.

The 2,000ft height is generally regarded as the difference between hill and mountain with the additional minimum 98.4ft drop giving a meaningful challenge of 30 mountains. In official mountain terminology they are known as Hewitts. The geographic area is clear, defined by the new boundary of the Yorkshire Dales National Park (as of 2016). However, as many of the mountains within the park are in Cumbria or Lancashire, I have referred to the area throughout the book as 'The Dales'.

The Dales is known as a wonderful area to walk but, aside from the famous 'Three Peaks', very little is known about the hills and mountains of the area. Many guide books describe the lovely riverside walks, walks that take in the history of the area and walks that showcase the wonderful rolling landscape.

However, very few people know anything about the mountains at all. It's a selective (or should I say odd) group that enters into a conversation about the merits of Rogan's Seat over Gragareth!

Of course many do know and talk about the Three Peaks of Yorkshire challenge. On any given Saturday from April to September the slopes of Pen-y-Ghent, Ingleborough and Whernside are crowded places. However the people embarking on this Three Peaks challenge are usually driven by the 'challenge' of completion, with the scenery being of only secondary consideration. As a guide I have on occasions come across people who have no idea where they are, not even aware that they are in Yorkshire.

The Dales 30 provides a completely different sort of challenge. A more leisurely challenge, one that can be completed at one's own pace, involve multiple visits, can be done at any time of the year (and should be) and one that covers most of the area. It brings with it a full appreciation of the Dales. The 30 mountains all display different characteristics, have different approaches and involve different challenges.

The Dales 30

The variety is down to geology and the underlying bedrock. The carboniferous limestone to the south and west of the area coupled with the thin soils bring a rockier landscape. Further north the shale and sandstone offer a smoother profile, deeper soils and a peat and heather clad moorland. Just contrast Pen-y -Ghent with Yockenthwaite Moor which lie only a few miles apart.

Travelling at different times of the year certainly adds to the enjoyment of the challenge. Buckden Pike in the snow is a very different proposition to a leisurely amble on a long summer's day. It brings a sense of adventure and excitement that, after many ascents, still gives me a thrill and at times a real burst of adrenalin. Between the two seasonal extremes lie the wonderful colours of autumn and the pretty flowers, lambs and freshness that a bright spring day can bring.

The Dales 30 will take you to the far corners of the Dales and to places you may not otherwise visit. The Dales 30 will bring you to the lesser spotted Dent, the book town of Sedbergh, exquisite Upper Swaledale and underrated Kirkby Stephen as well as the more popular villages in Upper Wharfedale, Ribblesdale and the queen of market towns, Hawes. Spending a weekend away in the Yorkshire Dales, climbing a couple of mountains and enjoying the evening in a traditional Dales pub surely ranks with the top weekend breaks in the world.

A day on Yarlside was typical for me. A late summer's day, warm hazy weather, an unclimbed hill and a new route. Just what I like! For half an hour I took the leisurely stroll along the Cautley valley enjoying the spectacular backdrop of Cautley Spout, a magnificent waterfall. A steep climb had me sweating on Yarlside before a gentle wind cooled me as the summit beckoned. For the next 45 minutes the going was perfect, easy walking on short, soft grass as I followed the undulating ridge to Randygill Top. From here I sat and worked out an unusual route down, enjoying virgin territory near Wandale Fell. I picked my way through sheep, farms and a quiet beck before emerging again at the Cross Keys Inn. I was happy to finish the walk with a pot of tea in this fascinating inn. Perfect.

Scotland has the Munros, the Lake District has the Wainwrights; let's hope the Dales 30 become as well known.

How to Use this Book

There are **30 mountains** in the book which breach the 2,000ft mountain threshold (the accepted height where a hill becomes a mountain). These are divided up into 20 'walks'. Some of the summits are easier to combine than to climb separately.

Each 'walk' in the book contains the following information:

A Personal View. An introductory section which offers my thoughts on the mountain, the best and worst features of the time I have spent on them and any personal experiences that may be entertaining.

Photography. I have included as many photos as possible. They were taken on my various visits to each mountain. One of the joys of the digital age is that an 'amateur' can take much better photos than in the past. I have tried to include photography from different times of the year to reflect the excellence of the Dales in all seasons.

Routes. I have described my 'Best Route' in some detail and this is my personal choice for climbing the mountain. A separate section 'Alternative Routes' offers other possibilities of ascent. One of the pleasures of climbing the Dales 30 is to try more than one route and have your own favourite.

Maps. I have designed some sketch maps which reflect the different routes. These are only an indication of route options and not a definitive route guide. Always transpose them on to one of the excellent maps that you can buy. I recommend the 1:25,000 Ordnance Survey Explorer series or the 'designed for walkers' Harvey maps.

Extra Information. I have added some small sections on other interesting facts of the mountain or nearby area which will bring more of a flavour to each mountain.

The core of the book describes the Dales 30 but I have added some different sections to enhance the read.

Outside Contributors. I have asked some specialists to write a short section on their areas of expertise; all involve climbing the mountains but from a different perspective to my own. For this I would like to thank Heather, Andy, Barry, Mark and Matt for their efforts.

Extra Fells. Height is not everything! A few of the most striking fells in the Dales are less than 2,000ft. On pages 112-115 I have described four of my personal favourites that lie within the National Park.

Books are limited by space and can only offer so much information. If you would like further information on the Dales 30 please visit the Where2walk website and search for the Dales 30.

Safety in the Mountains

The Dales 30 involve climbing the highest mountains in Yorkshire, Lancashire and some remote spots in Cumbria. Much of the upper areas are trackless, the terrain underfoot can be poor and exhausting, rivers can provide dangerous crossings in spate and it is easy to become disorientated when the cloud comes down. Winter conditions are particularly dangerous; short days, frozen ground and snow slowing progress are typical difficulties.

This book is intended to be only a rough guide to the best routes up the mountains and not used as a 'one stop shop'.

Anyone climbing the Dales 30 should be able to navigate using a map and compass. A GPS can be used as an aid to a map and compass but not as a replacement. Mobile phones can also help but they are easily damaged, run out of battery and it is not always possible to get a signal.

Appropriate clothing should be worn and, if walking on your own, a second person informed of your route and likely return time. In groups always plan for the slowest member of the party. If you do ever get into serious trouble call 999 or 112 and ask for the Mountain Rescue.

Not only do these precautions help reduce (but not eliminate) any dangers, they will make the walks much more enjoyable.

Three Peaks Project

Friends of
THE THREE PEAKS
YORKSHIRE DALES

Having enjoyed the mountains of the Dales 30 you may like to put something back. Any donation to the Friends of the 3 Peaks Project will be used by the national Park to help improve the paths and signage.

Howgills

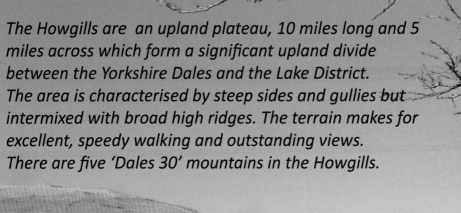

The Howgills are an upland plateau, 10 miles long and 5 miles across which form a significant upland divide between the Yorkshire Dales and the Lake District.
The area is characterised by steep sides and gullies but intermixed with broad high ridges. The terrain makes for excellent, speedy walking and outstanding views.
There are five 'Dales 30' mountains in the Howgills.

The Calf
Calders   2,216ft (675m)

2,218ft (676m)

Cautley Spout

Key Details (My Best Route)

Distance:	18km (11 miles)
Height to Climb:	740m (2,430ft)
O/S Explorer Map:	OL19 Howgills & Eden Valley
Parking:	SD 659922 Sedburgh, Car Park.

My View

Pick up The Calf and place it on the other side of the M6 and it would become nearly as popular as the Langdale Pikes and Helvellyn...it is that good. Fortunately it remains stoically to the east of the M6 and safely away from the crowds.

The Calf is the highest point in the Howgills and the most sought after summit for those in the area. There is an added appeal of having the highest cascade waterfall in England (650ft high) on its flanks.

The Calf (and its satellite summit Calders) are graceful peaks with steep sides and rolling ridges. The walking is easy and the views outstanding. I originally climbed The Calf from the Cross Keys Inn to the west but can happily say, that as good as this route is, the one that comes direct from Sedbergh is better. There is more ridge walking, more appreciation of the scale of the Howgills and the bonus of a circular walk which finishes alongside the River Rawthey.

I recently completed a day on The Calf (from Sedbergh) in perfect winter conditions. The ground was frozen, the skies a deep blue and there was a thin layer of snow accumulated on the eastern facing slopes. The steep climb up Winder took no time at all and the walk from Winder to The Calf was utterly delightful. The Lakeland fells were dramatically laid out to the west with the more rounded Pennines to the north and east, a true panorama of all that is good about this part of England.

Summit of The Calf

The Calf

My Best Route
(from Sedbergh)

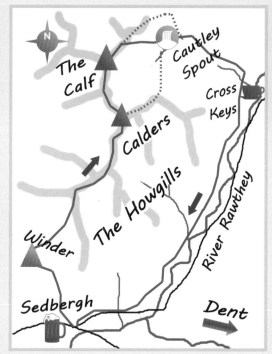

1.   From the Dalesman Inn follow Howgill Lane past the school and along the tarmac road for 300m. Turn north to Lockbank Farm, pass through the farm on to open fellside. This is an excellent path that zig zags uphill to the fine summit of Winder at 473m.

2.   Head north east from Winder on a good track past Arant Haw and Rowentree Grains for nearly 3km (gradually turning in a more northerly direction). A steep climb finishes at the summit of Calders.

3.   The Calf is only 1km away just west of north on an easy gradient path. From here the full scale of the Howgills is laid out (views permitting!) including the vast expanse of rarely visited land to the north. Open up your map and enjoy.

4.   From the summit head north east for 0.5km and then east on a footpath leading into the head of Cautley Spout. A rough path follows the north side of the stream until the valley floor is reached, joining a footpath coming down from Bowderdale on your left.

River Rawthey

5. Follow the footpath south east until it divides just before the Rawthey River. A bridlepath (becoming more of a farm track) then contours the side of the Howgill Fells heading south with the Rawthey River on your left and below. After 3km the path meets a tarmacked lane at Thunsgill Farm. Follow this lane into Sedbergh.

Near Winder

An Excellent Alternative

(The Cross Keys Inn) 11.5km/7 miles

1.   From the Cross Keys Inn cross the River Rawthey and head SW for 0.5km before turning NNW. Keep to the north side of the river heading towards the waterfall of Cautley Spout. After 1km the path splits, take the left hand fork that climbs steeply by the waterfall. Rather than carry on straight towards The Calf, I prefer leaving the path and heading south along the top of the Cautley cliffs (keeping them to your left) until reaching the minor summit of Great Dummack.

2.   Head WSW from Great Dummack for 750m to Calders, then north for 1km on a good path to the summit of The Calf. To vary the descent route and provide an alternative view of Cautley Spout, head NE on a bridleway for 2km until it reaches the col of Bowderdale, a lonely spot. From here turn SE and follow a path back towards the foot of Cautley Spout. This is the right hand fork of the ascent route; follow the outbound path back to the Cross Keys Inn.

Sedbergh, England's Book Town

Sedbergh is one of only two Book Towns in England (Atherstone is the other, a recent development) and a member of the International Organisation of Book Towns. A browse amongst the shops usually unearths some gems.

Hay on Wye in Wales may be more famous but the choice of second hand book shops in Sedbergh makes this market town worth a visit.

Alternative Approaches

From the East and the North

The distances are long and described in the climbs of Yarlside and Fell Head.

A Howgill crossing (including The Calf and Calders)

A very enjoyable walk if you have a car at each end. This route is described on pages 26-27.

Fell Head

2,099ft (640m)

Key Details (My Best Route)

Key Details (My Best Route)

Distance:	8km (5 miles)
Height to Climb:	465m (1,525ft)
O/S Explorer Map:	OL19 Howgills & Eden Valley
Parking:	SD 630979 Fairmile Beck, Howgill Lane, Off Road

My View

Another excellent walk in the Howgills. Fell Head is the western Howgill equivalent of Yarlside. It has an intricate network of graceful, grassy ridges; the walking is a delight on excellent turf and there are outstanding views. Fell Head has the advantage over Yarlside in having better views of the Lake District and a great perspective of the Lune Valley (only partially disturbed by the M6). However, the summit is not as well formed and graceful.

I have glanced up at Fell Head and its satellites (although I have never known its name) for many years as I've swept past on the M6. The paths networking the steep fellside are clearly visible and have distracted me on many occasions; where do they go, who uses them (walkers or just used by the local farmers) and for what purpose. It was only when I realised that Fell Head was one of the Dales 30 that I had a good reason to head up the Howgills from the west. In all the years of driving past I had never seen anyone on the paths so I was surprised when I followed a couple up from Howgill Lane and then dumbfounded when I discovered two more people ticking the summit having crossed over from The Calf. It's a secret business this fell walking.

We were the lucky ones, a lovely walk (I actually extended it on the undulating ridge to The Calf and back) in a beautiful and neglected part of England.

Start at Fairmile Beck

Fell Head

My Best Route

(from Howgill Lane)

1.   There is limited parking on Howgill Lane, however just to the north of Fairmile Beck there is a cleared place for a number of cars. An isolated tree stump marks the spot.

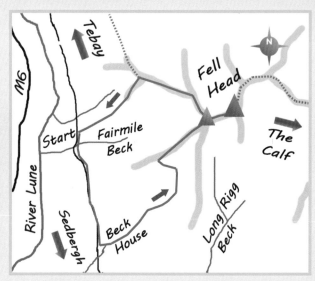

2. Walk south for 2km on Howgill Lane to a lane heading east at Beck House. After fiddling through the farmyard (there are signs directing you) and passing through three gates, cross the stream and head for the final 'fell wall'.

3. Beyond the gate on the fell wall the public footpath gradually climbs north of east for 750m though open fellside. When a path emerges from your right turn north to a small stream. From the stream climb WNW to the start of the ridge of Whins End.

4.   From Whins End the grassy ridge climbs steeply ENE to the west top of Fell Head and the best place for views of the Lake District. 200m further east is the true summit marked by a fair sized cairn. The ridge to The Calf carries on initially in the same direction before bending and climbing in a south easterly direction. It is 2km away.

5.   From the summit of Fell Head return to the west top and head north west for 1.5km to the high point of Ling Haw. Carry on for a further 100m then drop steeply south west directly to the car.

I was pleasantly surprised to be joined by some wild ponies on the descent, I had only seen them on the east side of the Howgills but maybe this is a different group.

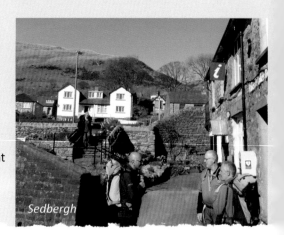

Sedbergh

Fell Head

Fell Head from Beck House

Dales Way and the Lune Valley

For six of its 128km the Dales Way follows the River Lune through the section of the Lune Valley to the west of the Howgills.

The Dales Way footpath is the best way of exploring the river and the valley of this forgotten area of the country.

Where the river bends at right angles, the 'Crook' of Lune, is often described as one of the most beautiful corners of England. Very few people know about this.

Fell Ponies

Fell Ponies are powerful and hardy and should not be thought of as at all 'horsey'. Pricked ears, kind eyes, a broad head and an alert nature characterise them.

The Howgills are one of the few places where they can be seen in the wild; the nature of the communal land of the area and lack of boundaries making it an ideal place for the packs to roam. The small numbers though make them susceptible to any disease or illness which could wipe them out very rapidly. They are a fine sight but vulnerable.

Alternative Routes

(From Carlingill Bridge)

The excellent track on the north facing shoulder, seen so clearly from the M6, meets the main descent path of the Best Route at Ling Haw and continues to the summit. There is no alternative descent unless returning to the car park on Howgill Lane 8km to the south. As with all the walks in the Howgills avoid climbing in the deep gullies and head for the much pleasanter ridges.

(From The Calf)

Most people add Fell Head directly from The Calf then return to the main ridge. This does not do justice to a fine peak in an unexplored corner of England.

Yarlside

2,096ft (639m)

Randygill Top 2,047ft (624m)

Yarlside

Key Details (My Best Route)

Distance:	10.5km (6.5 miles)
Height to Climb:	690m (2,265ft)
O/S Explorer Map:	OL19 Howgills & Eden Valley
Parking:	SD 698969 Cross Keys Inn, Off Road.

My View

Yarlside is an absolute cracker of a mountain. Any approach entails a steep climb but each is well rewarded on reaching the neat summit, perched on a grassy dome of land. Sitting next to the cairn feels like a seat with the gods but, more practically, Yarlside offers the best perspective to study the topography of the Howgills. To the north is wild country with the rolling hills gradually dropping into the Lune Valley. One of these rolling hills is another, exceptional viewpoint of Randygill Top.

The deep divide of Bowderdale separates Yarlside from the southern and western Howgills but even in this direction the views are excellent. The main spine of the Howgills is clearly outlined to the south, with The Calf and Calders, prominant. Look west and an enjoyable exercise of Wainwright spotting can be indulged in (including a splendid view of Great Gable) whilst to the east there are views over Wild Boar Fell, Baugh Fell and the remote Pennine massif.

Even though Cautley Spout cannot be spotted from the summit, the crags of Cautley can. On the climb (and the main walk described below should certainly be taken in a clockwise direction) the views of Cautley Spout cannot be bettered from any other vantage point. Extending the walk to Randygill Top only adds to the pleasure. Pick a nice day.

Cautley Spout, Yarlside on the right

Yarlside

My Best Route *(from the Cross Keys Inn)*

1.   There is some limited parking on the A683 at the Cross Keys Inn but if this is full there is more extensive parking 1km north. From the Cross Keys drop steeply down to the River Rawthey, cross the footbridge and join the bridleway initially heading SW. A footpath

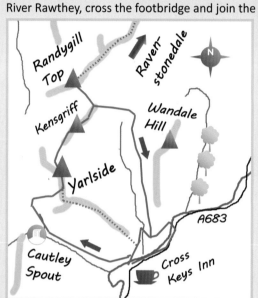

heads NW after 300m and into the valley of Cautley Beck. The great waterfall of Cautley Spout is now in view, the largest of its kind in England and a constant companion on your walk to the col at Bowderdale Head.

2.   As Cautley Spout is approached the path splits; take the right hand fork that goes NNW up a steep path heading away from Cautley Spout. When the gradient flattens out at Bowderdale Head look for a path skirting the hillside to your right and then climbing steeply on the south side of a stream. This is a steep 250m climb but unavoidable. A col is reached, turn north and a further 50m brings the lovely summit of Yarlside.

3.   To add Randygill Top head north. Kensgriff is a steep sided hill between Yarlside and Randygill Top. From the col which lies to the NE of Kensgriff head NW to the summit of Randygill Top. If the cloud is high the views north are excellent and unusual. Return SE to the col for the descent.

4.   From the col aim east and a steep grassy descent drops 150m (no track) before crossing a stream. Climb 40m east to a path (it circles Wandale Hill). Follow this south for 2km to the farm at Narthwaite. If conditions are dry take the path steeply down to cross Backside Beck (no footbridge) and rejoin the bridleway leading to the Cross Keys. If the conditions are wet, follow the farm access track east to where it meets the A683 1km north of the Cross Keys. Return along the road for a pleasant cup of coffee.

Cross Keys Inn

Yarlside

Alternative Routes

(From Ravenstonedale in the North)
18.5km (*11.5 miles*)

A full day's walk in a rarely visited part of the area (now included within the National Park's protection). I have never seen a soul whilst walking here.

There are alternative routes from the north in the lower half of the walk that all meet at Green Bell. Best to head up a farm track which skirts the Knott and on the descent from Green Bell return further to the west, meeting the road at Tranmoor.

From Green Bell the walk over Randygill Top all the way to Yarlside is on excellent turf but steep (Randygill Top is, however, easily skirted on the return). Return the same way.

(Just Yarlside, excluding Randygill Top)

Cross Keys is the best start point. However, after reaching the summit via Bowderdale col take the direct route down the SE shoulder leading directly to the River Rawthey and the start.

Cross Keys Inn

I used to visit the Cross Keys Inn as a small boy in the 1970s to have 'tea' but it was only recently I returned. We had bacon and eggs. It is still excellent with bags of character and historical interest.

As a Temperance Inn there is no alcohol served but the food is very good all day and if you are after just a cup of tea and cake you can sit in comfy chairs and enjoy the relaxed atmosphere of days gone by.

The Northern Howgills

The Northern Howgills are rarely visited either by farmers or walkers; it is the land of sheep and moorland. At its foot are two of the most pleasant little villages in the area, Ravenstonedale and Newbiggin on Lune. Pretty churches, good quality pubs and a thriving local community all exist in harmony.

The River Lune has its source in these hills (above Newbiggin) before it heads west and then north, circling two full sides of the Howgill Fells.

The Northern Howgills are part of the new extended Yorkshire Dales National Park.

Crossing the Howgills

I have only ever once made a full south to north crossing of the Howgills. I was joined by Debbie and Andy North who run the impressive 'Access TOG' project which helps people with mobility difficulties enjoy the fells of Britain. Andy takes up the story....

The idea of traversing the Howgills from Sedbergh up to Bowderdale Head formed a section of an accessible long-distance trek from Semerwater to Ullswater and finally onto Bassenthwaite in the Lake District. On paper it seemed straightforward enough. As we were taking an all-terrain wheelchair with us (ATW), a TerrainHopper, we knew it would be wise to travel mob-handed. The group consisted of the two of us, two innocent bystanders, Rachel Briggs from the Yorkshire Dales National Park Authority and Jonathan, our erstwhile 'go to' guy.

On the morning of the trek, we were told we'd never get the ATW up Winder because "it's too bloody steep". Looking at what we could see of it as we set off, the warning rang true. Winder was shrouded in cloud.

Nevertheless, we climbed to the summit and laid hands on the trig point, 473m above sea level. It was a steep climb on a clear grassy track. Our main difficulty at this point - apart from trying to move and breathe at the same time - was that the wheels on the ATW struggled to grip in places. It really was very wet.

We deliberated at the trig point for two blinks of an eye about whether we should continue to The Calf. We did. Again, the track was easy to follow, wide and skirted some summits which Jonathan assured us were there. We just climbed higher into the clouds. The rain got heavier and heavier. Every now and again the wind would swirl the clouds a little and a delicious view down steep-sided fells would open up.

10 miles

The push up to Calders was steep and extremely wet. The track was easy enough to follow, we were just being teased by cloud and rain. After Calders, we dropped a little into a col before a final easy push onto the summit of The Calf, 676m above sea level. With an ATW. In spite of the dreadful conditions, we were delighted. It was eery and I could imagine on my own it being scary but to us it was exhilarating.

The route then went via Hazelgill Knott. Here, the track we followed is easy to miss if you're not on your mettle, the key turn to the north is by a couple of lonely tarns. The plan was to contour around onto West Fell before descending to Bowderdale Head. An arduous undertaking. The batteries of the ATW were practically flat - to this day we have no idea how it kept going - and everybody hit the dirt at least once. Anyone who says they didn't is lying.

Again, we caught brief glimpses of the Howgills, the cloud parting every so often to show enticing views. Our main regret from the whole traverse was that we didn't get enough of them; but we will be back when the weather's better.

Why? Because what we did see whetted our appetites for a totally different experience up in the Howgills. A dry one. With views.

And whilst our day was shrouded in cloud and sodden in rain, it was the day from the whole trek the entire group still talks about even if it is accompanied by a wry smile.

Cumbrian Pennines

North of the Yorkshire Dales and east of the Howgills lie a series of deep valleys overlooked by vast expanses of upland moorland. The walking can be tough as the miles are long and much of it is over trackless moors and peat hags but the rewards in terms of solitude and silence more than compensate.
There are five 'Dales 30' mountains in the Cumbrian Pennines.

Wild Boar Fell

Baugh Fell

Key Details (My Best Route)

Distance:	18km (11 miles)
Height to Climb:	560m (1,840ft)
O/S Explorer Map:	OL19 Howgills & Eden Valley
Parking:	SD 713979 Rawthey Bridge, Off Road.

The Shelter

My View

Baugh Fell is perfect for navigation training! The vast plateau is featureless and the domain of sadistic Duke of Edinburgh instructors, fell runners on the Sedbergh Wilson Run and the army. Walkers rarely visit, put off by grim warnings of bog and hard going. Baugh Fell is a large expanse of fellside which lies in Cumbria sandwiched between the elegant Howgills and the striking valleys of Garsdale and Upper Mallerstang; Wild Boar Fell is its twin peak.

The summit area has a number of tarns, a splendid vantage point and some striking views to the west in particular. Sheep tracks though will lead you astray and into some of the wettest ground that you will come across in the Dales 30. I have not found Baugh Fell difficult at all but legend has it that this is the boggiest fell around. Don't be put off.

I have attempted Baugh Fell on a few occasions but only actually reached the high point (which is not the trig at Knoutberry Haw shown opposite) once. There is little doubt that the route from Rawthey Bridge has the most variety and is the most satisfactory. I thoroughly enjoyed exploring Rawthey Gill (it really does feel like you are in a lost world), finding the lonely shelter below Knoutberry Haw and then emerging on to the plateau near the summit. The views over the Howgills complete a splendid round.

Knoutberry Haw

Baugh Fell

My Best Route

(from Rawthey Bridge)

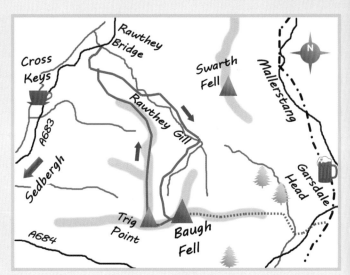

1.　　There are no public rights of way on Baugh Fell, a footpath (part of Wainwight's Pennine Journey) skirts the northern flanks of the mountain but that is it. The remainder of the mountain is Open Access Land giving you the right to roam (see page 33). Paths when they do appear are unreliable and may be just sheep tracks.

2.　　The footpath leading directly into Rawthey Gill is difficult to follow. I gave it a shot and ended up lost, not one of my better moments but it was confusing. Better to head SW from the bridge along the 'Street' for 500m and join a bridleway heading SSE on the south side of the valley. Follow this 2km to the waterfalls of Uldale, cross the river and carry on its north side for 2.5km heading SE.

3.　　Leave the path and turn SSW

into Rawthey Gill (trackless), then cross it. For once it is better to walk close to the stream itself. The sides are steep and the terrain difficult. Continue on its east bank for 500m to Gill Head, before a steep climb SSE brings you to a well constructed shelter (737924, see page 30).

4.　　Take a bearing SSE past East Tarns to the summit of Tarn Rigg Hill, it's tricky in poor visibility to hit the highest point but at least a solid wall marks the point where you can go no further. Head west and then WNW for 1km along the wall to the trig point at Knoutberry Haw.

5.　　From the trig point head north for 1.5km to West Baugh Fell Tarn, losing very little height in the process. From here a sketchy path heads north turning NW as it drops gradually for over 3km to the small rise of Bluecaster. The Howgills dominate the view. Skirt Bluecaster on its eastern flanks and rejoin the outbound route near the 'Street' and a short walk NE to Rawthey Bridge.

Baugh Fell

Howgills from Baugh Fell

Access Land

In a nutshell Open Access Land provides the right to roam in much of our privately owned upland areas. Whereas on lower lands access through private land is either via a public right of way (footpath or bridleway) or with the landowner's express permission, on upland areas the CROW (Countryside Right of Way) Act of 2000 offers considerably more freedom to walkers.

There are over three million acres of Open Access Land in England and Wales including most of the upland moors near the summits of the Dales 30 (example of Baugh Fell with its limited public rights of way).

There are some, usually temporary, restrictions during the grouse shoot (particularly for those with dogs) but in general it offers a freedom that was not there prior to the Act.

In practice walking on trackless moorland is not that pleasant and is often very hard work. However over time walkers' paths start to appear which often aid access to the summits of the mountains. These are usually faint and intermittent but will improve over time.

Alternative Routes

(Garsdale)

The best option is to park (or better still hop off the train) at Garsdale Head, cross the road and take the path heading NNW for 500m to Clough Force. From here walk in a general westerly direction along the north side of the wall for 4km to the summit. It is remote country but the wall makes it very difficult to get lost.

Return the same way.

Any other shorter approaches from Garsdale are fraught with access difficulties and rough ground. I would recommend not attempting Baugh Fell from anywhere west of Garsdale Station.

Wild Boar Fell

2,323ft (708m)

Swarth Fell 2,234ft (681m)

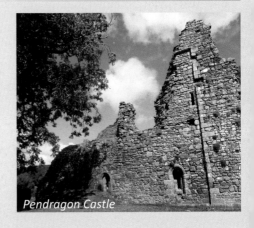
Pendragon Castle

Key Details (My Best Route)

Distance:	20km (12.5 miles)
Height to Climb:	620m (2,035ft)
O/S Explorer Map:	OL19 Howgills & Eden Valley
Parking:	SD 798927 Moorcock Inn, a mile from Garsdale Station.

My View

Wild Boar Fell is a proper mountain, anyone who takes on the day will reflect on an interesting but hard one. The lower slopes tend to be the hardest work (steeper and muddier) whilst 'up top' has the easiest walking. However, if the cloud is down then easiest becomes challenging and a compass essential on the featureless plateau.

The approaches from Mallerstang are limited, a bridleway (the Pennine Journey) does skirt the northern slopes but further south and closer to Swarth Fell any descent is mainly trackless and rough. It is why I can thoroughly recommend the 'Best Route', a full north to south crossing making use of the Settle to Carlisle railway. As well as the advantages of an A to B walk, the crossing makes use of the better terrain, has consistently excellent views and ends conveniently near one of the best pubs in the Dales (Moorcock Inn at Garsdale Head).

As with the fells across Mallerstang there are many legends and mysteries surrounding Wild Boar Fell. The series of large cairns on the summit plateau overlooking Mallerstang could have been built for one of any number of reasons (I always like the idea of them scaring off invaders but I suspect it is more mundane). Similarly the name Wild Boar Fell is allegedly due to the mountain being home to the last 'wild boar'. Its tusk does lie in the church at Kirkby Stephen but, again, this may or may not be true...however, it is a striking name and that can only be good.

Large cairns on Wild Boar Fell

Wild Boar Fell

My Best Route

(via the Settle to Carlisle Railway)

1.　　Park near the Moorcock Inn not Garsdale Station. It is 1.5km away and a tedious 20 minutes but best out of the way early. Walk along the road towards Sedbergh for 50m and take the footpath heading south and signed to Garsdale Station. The trains are (at time of going to print) every two hours and there is one scheduled at the very civilised time of 9.20am.

2.　　On the train the nine miles are covered in 12 minutes and on arrival at Kirkby Stephen Station (not close to the town) head south for 3km on the A685/A683 to Tommy Road. If the road is a concern it is possible to leave it after 750m (just south of the road junction) on a side road. After another 500m a bridleway heads south for 2km to rejoin Tommy Road (a second minor road). This option is slower, wetter but safer.

3.　　On Tommy Road head east then south. Where the road bends east again head directly south on a farm track over Access Land. Climbing steadily the track disappears after 1.5km near two small tarns and some marshy land. Carry on south over steeper ground to Little Fell and then the route gradually drops for

1km, initially joining a wall and then to a junction with a major path heading east west.

4.　　Climb steadily south on a faint path to the plateau of Wild Boar Fell. The plateau is 1.5km long and worth exploring. The high point (trig and shelter) is to the west, the standing stones to the south and east. However, the path to Swarth Fell is to the south and follows a fence to the col and then a wall to its summit.

5.　　The first large cairn is the summit of Swarth Fell but carry on following the wall SSE past a second cairn 1km distant (great views to the south) and then dropping down over often wet hillside. Follow the wall for 3km as it gradually bends SE until it meets a footpath heading east. This leads to a footbridge over the railway on to the road and a short walk south to the Moorcock Inn.

Wild Boar Fell

Wild Boar Fell from the south

Pendragon Castle, Mallerstang

I came across Pendragon Castle on a hot summer's day and was entranced immediately. Almost certainly built in the 12th century in a Norman architectural style, Pendragon Castle has housed many famous inhabitants including Lady Anne Clifford. Today it is in ruins, but interesting ruins with the peace and tranquillity of its location making it a perfect picnic spot.

Sadly though there is no direct evidence it was the castle of King Arthur's father, beloved of legend. Despite the lack of evidence many believe it may have been.

Further north a second ruined castle sits alone in a large green field. This is Lammerside Castle which surprisingly (and sadly) has no legends attached to it!

Rabbits

Deemed a luxury in times past, rabbits were introduced to the Mallerstang area in Norman times and once they had adapted to our climate became a luxury during the middle ages. The fur made soft clothing and footwear, the meat was tasty and their stomachs provided rennet for some cheeses. They are not native to the UK.

Most Popular Route

(From the Thang) 8 miles/13km

There is parking at the Thang, 1km north from where the Pennine Bridleway heads west up Wild Boar Fell. At a junction of walls, following a 2km climb, head south along a good path to the summit plateau of Wild Boar Fell. The highest point has a trig point to the west of the large summit plateau.

From the trig point follow a fence SSW for 1km along the plateau, south for 500m to the col and tarn and then south for a further 750m to the big cairn marking the summit of Swarth Fell. Head SSE for 1km to the southern cairn of Swarth Fell.

A few metres beyond the summit leave the fence at an intermittent path that heads east and then ENE towards Aisgill Moor Cottages and the road. It is nearly 5km walk back to the car.

If climbing just Wild Boar Fell it is easiest and most sensible to return via the way of ascent.

High Seat

2,326ft (709m)

Little Fell   2,188ft (667m)

Blades Bridge

Key Details (My Best Route)

Distance:	16km (10 miles)
Height to Climb:	470 m (1,540ft)
O/S Explorer Map:	OL19 Howgills & Eden Valley
Parking:	SD 778964 Aisgill Cottages, Off Road.

My View

I had walked the lower slopes of both fells a number of times before collecting the two summits. It is a place of legend, myths and other downright lies. Dick Turpin never did leap the bridge at Hell Gill, King Arthur may or may not have visited Pendragon Castle (owned for a while by his father...probably) and the Scots did not stop here in terror when they saw the standing stones of Wild Boar Fell. What is true is that within a mile or so of Hell Gill Bridge is the source of three great English rivers; the Eden, the Swale and the Ure.

As with many mountains in the area, the approaches to the summits from every direction are hard work. However, the higher, broader ridges offer better terrain and enjoyable walking. It is undulating land, never dropping too far and covering some superb places including Gregory Chapel and its fine currick (long cairn), Hugh Seat (named after Hugh de Morville, a knight of Pendragon) and Lady's Pillar (named for Lady Anne Clifford). A proper history lesson.

I prefer the approach from Aisgill Cottages and walking north along the ridge; the views into the remote Pennines are excellent and the descent along The Riggs avoids much of the peat hags lower down. However, the route from Outhgill does include a better perspective of Mallerstang Edge. Both are described. I would finally add that this is compass country, ignore that advice at your peril!

Wild Boar Fell from Little Fell

High Seat

My Best Route

(from Aisgill Cottages)

1.   Parking is available at Aisgill Moor Cottages. Follow the footpath from the south of the cottages, over the railway bending left and then NE on a farm track through the farm at Hell Gill and 200m further to the famous bridge. It is a good spot and full of legend.

2.   From the bridge keep to the south of the stream on an initially very faint path, climbing steadily on some rough ground. A cairn can be clearly seen just north of east, 1.5m distant. Aim for it. The path in the upper reaches is intermittent, best just to pick the soundest ground. From the cairn the land flattens and the small cairn of Little Fell soon appears. This is the highest point but head

Source of the Eden

750m south to the cairn at Sails with some excellent views south into the heart of the Dales

3.   Return to Little Fell and join a rough path that meets a fence at Scarth of Scaith after 750m. Keep to the fence for 1km to Hugh Seat and then follow the upland tracks that keep to the highest ground in a general northerly direction. From Hugh Seat it is nearly 3km to High Seat including the short climb to Gregory Chapel and the final short pull to the summit. There are three small cairns on the summit plateau, the highest one is towards the northern end but not the largest cairn.

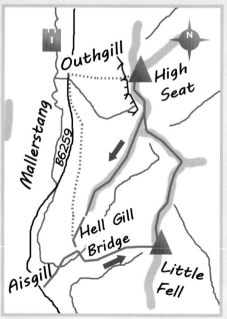

4.   From the summit I headed west to the top of Mallerstang Edge and enjoyed following the rim as it winds south. After 2km the edge becomes a broad shoulder of High Rigg. Keep to the high part of the shoulder and head SSW. The views are interesting, particularly over Wild Boar Fell and the railway as the shoulder gradually drops to Hell Gill Bridge. From here follow the footpath back to Aisgill Cottages and the start.

Hell Gill Bridge

Hell Gill Bridge was built in 1825 (replacing an earlier bridge) and overlooks the deep divide of Hell Gill.

Whilst not exactly "striketh a certain horror" as described by William Cambden in the 16th Century it is impressive.

From near this point the Ure heads east to the North Sea and the Eden west to the Irish Sea, a true watershed. The River Swale also has its origins nearby.

Lady Anne Clifford

An extraordinary woman of the 17th Century, Lady Anne inherited the vast family estate at the age of 43 after protracted legal wranglings (in the age when women were reckoned not able to manage pretty much anything).

From then till her death aged 86 she managed and improved much of the estate including Pendragon, Skipton, Brough and Appleby Castles. She was also an artist, literary figure and all round good egg. There is even a 'Lady Anne's Way' long distance footpath.

Alternative Routes

(From Outhgill) 9 miles

Head past the outdoor centre and onto the open fellside. Use a cairn high on Mallerstang Edge as a marker and head generally east, but there is no path (as marked on the map) so the going is difficult. Choose a route through the Edge but all will involve a very steep, short pull before the simple stroll to the summit of High Seat.

From the summit head south for 5km on the undulating ridge to Little Fell. Drop directly west from Little Fell over some rough ground to Hell Gill Bridge. An excellent bridleway then leads north all the way to the road near Outhgill.

These two fells can be done separately but the pleasures lie on the broad long ridge between them. Both climbs are over rough ground.

High Seat from the west

A Schoolboy's Memories

Barry, my eldest brother, spent his school years at the formidable Sedbergh School in the heart of the Cumbrian Fells. Fell running was his hobby and inspired the love he now has for the mountains. Here are some of his thoughts...

Cautley Beck

During the winter months a visitor could be forgiven for thinking that Sedbergh, with its surrounding school buildings, was a somewhat austere place. However, that was not how I saw it during my school years in the early 1970s. My world was dominated by the hills and the valleys. Winder looked over the town from the north, Frostrow and the river Rawthey lay to the south and mighty Baugh Fell dominated the eastern skyline. Nearly every day during those winter terms of 1972 and 1973 we were out running over the fells and along the riverside paths.

I was a member of the school cross country running team. On successive weeks two of of our best runners, Straker and Sawday, broke the school record on Sedbergh's home course over the Frostrow fells. But our sights were set on the Wilson Run, the famous Sedbergh ten mile course over some of the roughest terrain imaginable.

It starts by scything along the side of the Howgills, the dip into Thrushgill made up of near vertical grass and mud on both sides of the stream. After passing Cautley the course traverses Baugh Fell, the boggy ground broken only by the deep trenches of Plantation and Hebblethwaite. Finally Danny Bridge appears and a long run to the finish, tired legs making those final miles a test of the fastest and fittest.

The mystique of the event was not only the brutal nature of the course but the fact that the record had not been broken since 1899. How could this be, was the course shorter in those days? Our running master assured us that the course was not shorter. We learnt that Pumphrey and Grandage, the winners in those distant days before World War One, were fitter and faster than those that followed them because they spent all their spare time roaming the fells.

Needless to say none of us broke the record in 1972 or 1973. It was to be another 20 years before Charles Sykes finally broke it in 1993 and in 2016 John Campbell knocked a further two seconds off the ten mile record.

Sedbergh

Today the race, which is always held on a Tuesday in March, continues to live up to its legendary reputation.

Whilst we were at Sedbergh, there would often be climbs up Winder, sometimes we would carry on to Higher Winder and The Calf. On one occasion three of us did the 'Blue Ribbon'; the ten mile course, then the three mile course and finally Winder.

My mates got into a 20 minute argument near the summit of Winder so our chances of a good time disappeared. The bizarre scene is etched on my memory to this day.

I would like to say that the school song (see below) was in our heads, at least occasionally. It wasn't, but we were true to its sentiments.

'For it isn't our ancient lineage
There are others as old as we
And it isn't our pious founders
Though we honour their memory
'Tis the hills that surround us
Unchanged since our days began
It is Cautley, Calf and Winder
That make the Sedbergh man.'

When we were at school we were told by visiting 'Old Boys' that we would see Sedbergh in a different light when we returned after our schooldays. They were right. I now regard Sedbergh as a stunning place and one of the best places for walking (not running any more!) in Britain. I like to walk up Winder, and on to The Calf, returning to the road via Cautley Spout, but there are many other possibilities. Next time I return I intend to walk over Baugh Fell and Wild Baugh Fell, because I have never been to their summits.

Northern Dales

Wensleydale and Swaledale conjour up visions of green valleys and pleasant moorland fells set admist a rolling landscape. The mountains of the Northern Dales do not disappoint; the walking is generally good, the views outstanding and the attraction of the villages make for a perfect start and finish to a day out.
There are six 'Dales 30' mountains in the Northern Dales.

Looking west from near Hawes

Rogan's Seat

2,205ft (672m)

Key Details (My Best Route)

Distance:	11km (7.5 miles)
Height to Climb:	450m (1,480ft)
O/S Explorer Map:	OL30 Yorkshire Dales North & Central
Parking:	NY 893012 Keld, Car Park.

Summit Cairn

My View

Not many hill walkers visit Rogan's Seat for pleasure, it is mainly a ticking exercise for peak baggers or a quick detour for those walking the Coast to Coast. The small cairn at the summit is surrounded by a great expanse of peat hags typical of the Pennines that lie to the north. It is not a great spot with the views seeming distant and almost insignificant due to the bleak foreground. This is a land for grouse shooting and as a result the wide landrover tracks which criss cross the area make access somewhat more straightforward.

My first visit to Rogan's Seat (and I doubt many have repeated the experience) was a late decision from the top of Gunnerside Gill, not a route I can really recommend. My stupidity was compounded by returning exactly the same way through the peat hags instead of using the landrover track that lies to the south of the summit and west of the gill.

However I was determined to enjoy Rogan's Seat just once and I certainly achieved this with a pleasant climb from Keld via Swinners Gill. Once on the plateau I made use of the landrover tracks. I carried on north from the summit cairn and down west towards East Gill. The return along East Gill was rough but I was not complaining; somehow a climb of Rogan's Seat should not be easy. All in all a tough day on the fells.

Catrake Force

Rogan's Seat

My Best Route *(from Keld)*

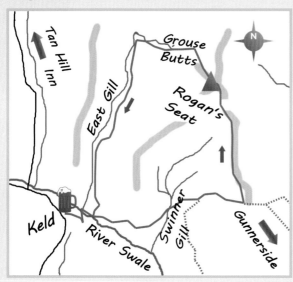

1. There is parking in the lovely hamlet of Keld. Take the bridleway next to the church heading SE, turn NE and cross the embryonic River Swale. Join the Pennine Way past Kisdon Force and follow the path SE for 500m. A footpath forks left and passes through the remains of Crackpot Hall, a two story house of legend and mystery. After Crackpot Hall the path bends NNE to remain well above Swinner Gill, then drops to a footbridge after 500m.

2. The path now heads east along the north bank of East Grain, passing some disused mining buildings, then climbs steeply out onto the moors. Join a landrover track on the moors and follow for a further 750m east to a gate and fence. Just past the gate the track divides, turn north and follow the track for 2km past some shooting butts and a small lodge to the high point. A small summit cairn with a pipe sticking out is 100m to the west perched on a peat hag.

3. Return to the track and continue north through a gate before turning west. The 'road' finishes in a turning circle, carry on the rutted track past more shooting butts. After the last butt the tracks become less used and rutted. Just prior to reaching East Gill the tracks turn SSW and start to contour the stream, roughly 30m below. The path is intermittent but keep to the contour (the stream becomes further away as it falls through a steep sided ravine). After 2km cross a fence (no stile) and as a second fence is approached the path becomes clearer and drops steeply before passing through the fence at a small gate.

Hay Meadows at Muker

4. From here the path is again clearer, eventually passing through a further gate and through a field, back to the bridleway above the River Swale. Keld is barely 10 minutes walk from here.

Keld

Alternative Routes

(From Gunnerside) 12km

A landrover track to the west of Gunnerside Gill makes a straightforward airy ascent of Rogan's Seat via the high moors. However the pleasure of climbing Rogan's Seat from Gunnerside lies in the gill itself where the industrial history of Swaledale can be explored at its best.

Be aware though, the crossing to Rogan's Seat from the north end of the gill is unpleasant in trackless peat hags.

The best way to solve the dilemma is to ascend to the landrover track up Blind Gill (footpath) from Gunnerside Gill, thereby enjoying much of its pleasures but not the final climb.

It is possible to vary the return to Gunnerside by turning west 2km from the summit and following a landrover track south above the River Swale.

Swinner Gill

The mountains and hillsides of Swaledale are rich in history. Lead mining transformed the landscape and today the bare rough slopes, ruined buildings and mines bear testament to rugged times in the 19th Century.

Swinner Gill is a very good example of this. Crackpot Hall was used at its core with the steep sided gill perfect for the thousands of miners to dig the precious lead from the hills. A walk through Upper Swaledale is always a fascinating lesson in history.

Rogan's Seat...the name

The name Rogan's Seat is over 1,000 years old and of Norse origin and apparently means Rogan's Upland Pasture. This is typical of Swaledale where places are named after people of times of yore.

There are also a number of 'seats' but these are spread through the Dales and include Lovely Seat, Ladies Seat, Citron Seat and Simon's Seat.

Great Knoutberry Hill 2,205ft (672m)

Key Details (My Best Route)

Distance:	11km (7 miles)
Height to Climb:	425m (1,405ft)
O/S Explorer Map:	OL2 Yorkshire Dales South & Western
Parking:	SD 771859 Bridge at Arten Gill, Off Road.

Arten Gill Viaduct

My View

Of the many thousands who skirt the flanks of Great Knoutberry on the Pennine Bridleway, (a companion route to the Pennine Way but one that can be completed by bike or horse), I would imagine only a handful of intrepid walkers take the shortish detour to its summit. In defence of the long distance traveller, most of the obvious attractions of the area are on the flanks of Great Knoutberry; the magnificent Arten Gill viaduct, Dent Station (the highest train station in England) and Widdale Tarns to name but a few.

However, there is no doubt in my mind that those who avoid the higher ground are missing out because Great Knoutberry Hill (or Widdale Fell as it is commonly known) is a wonderful place to spend an hour or two (weather permitting). The views down Dentdale are unsurpassed. There is an interesting array of finely built cairns overlooking the valley (reminiscent of the more famous ones on Nine Standards Rigg) but for what purpose it is difficult to know.

The views in all directions are excellent but it is the solitude that I always enjoy. I have never seen anyone on my frequent visits to the summit (Only Debbie North and Mist have ever accompanied me); it is skylarks and lapwings that provide the company.

Great Knoutberry Hill

Near Cowgill

Great Knoutberry Hill

My Best Route *(from Upper Dentdale)*

1.   The best option to park is beside the bridge at the foot of Arten Gill (on the west side) in Upper Dentdale, although Cowgill and the Sportsman's Inn provide alternatives.

2.   Cross the bridge and head east up a lane/bridleway, past some houses, towards the imposing Arten Gill viaduct. An information post explains some of the history of the viaduct, in particular the use of Dent marble in its construction. The path passes the viaduct on its north side before climbing steadily for 1.5km up Arten Gill Beck. Do not take the Pennine Bridleway (signed) but carry on for another 200m to a stile on a wall corner at the high point of the col.

3.   An intermittent path winds its way NNW up the fellside, keeping close to the wall on its west side but not always next to it. There are boggy stretches (but nothing unpleasant) which is why the path is intermittent. The wall bends to the NW before arriving at the double cairned summit, the lower of the two protected by a fence and facing Widdale.

4.   From the summit cairn head west whilst remaining on the southern side of the fence. The path is at best patchy as it gradually drops towards the Pennine Bridleway, one notable feature being a set of well constructed cairns which were built by someone with taste, as the views down Dentdale are spectacular. On meeting the bridleway turn north and follow it to the tarmacked road from Dentdale to Garsdale.

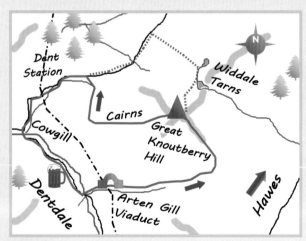

5.   Magnificent views of Dentdale distract from the road walking, as does a quick excursion to Dent Station (the highest in England). After 2km the road leads into the attractive hamlet of Cowgill. Turn left at the junction and follow the River Dee to Arten Gill and the car. If you are lucky the Sportsman's Inn may be open but the hours are restricted midweek.

Great Knoutberry Hill

Summit of Great Knoutberry Hill

Alternative Routes

There is in fact very little alternative to this walk. The bridleway on the approach up Arten Gill does carry on to Widdale and eventually Hawes but this is a poor route with no alternative ascent.

On the Best Route there is a possible excursion via Widdale Tarns from the summit rather than drop to the bridleway. It is a lovely situation but the walking is rough and trackless.

Dent Marble

Dentdale is the home of Dent Marble, not traditional marble but a form of untreated dark limestone with a high fossil concentrate. Its primary use was for fireplaces. From roughly 1800 it was used in all kinds of buildings, including the two viaducts in Dentdale, and can be seen today throughout the valley.

It is at the foot of Arten Gill, where the walk starts, that Dentdale had its one and only marble works factory.

The Bracken Way

There are a number of different long distance footpaths that pass through or are in the Yorkshire Dales but, in my opinion, the best is the new Bracken Way.

Not yet waymarked, the trail passes along the bridleway to the east and south of Great Knoutberry Fell into Dentdale via the Arten Gill viaduct (with a suggested option to climb Great Knoutberry Fell...obviously!).

Prior to this the Bracken Way passes through Malham, Upper Wharfedale, Aysgarth, Askrigg and Hawes amongst other wonderful Dales scenery. From Dent the route climbs Whernside and follows the higher or lower lands to Settle via Ingleton.

In total it is an 85 mile/137km walk taking seven days. There is even an opportunity to extend the walk by a few days by heading into Swaledale from Hawes.

The full details of the walk are found on the Where2walk website.

Great Shunner Fell 2,349ft (716m)

Lovely Seat 2,214ft (675m)

Key Details (My Best Route)

Distance:	19km (11.5 miles)
Height to Climb:	680m (2,230ft)
O/S Explorer Map:	OL30 Yorkshire Dales North & Central
Parking:	SD 867912 Hardraw near Green Dragon, Road side.

Burtersett

My View

The imposing presence of Great Shunner Fell (the third highest mountain of the Dales 30) is visited many times by long distance walkers taking on the Pennine Way. For them it's a taster of what's to come, the remote Pennine chain providing the long distance trail's greatest challenge. By contrast its neighbour, Lovely Seat, is rarely visited. In recent years Lovely Seat has been badly neglected but I find it an enjoyable hill. It has great views on the long descent towards Hawes and the added pleasure of a genuine 'Lovely Seat' on the summit (albeit not very comfortable).

Either by chance or design I have always treated Great Shunner Fell as a 'winter hill', three of my four climbs having been in winter conditions. The first time we didn't reach the summit due to some inept map reading, but two subsequent winter visits have been in good winter conditions, the hard ground increasing both the speed of the walk and its enjoyment. On my third visit I continued across to Lovely Seat, a bit of a trawl in the boggy ground near Buttertubs, but once on Lovely Seat the views were fantastic, Wensleydale shimmering in the winter light.

The route described from Hardraw is my favourite. The vast horseshoe feels aesthetically pleasing, the climb up Lovely Seat not too bad and the views seem better than climbing from the north. However, a second route from Swaledale in the north is also described.

Great Shunner Fell

Great Shunner and Lovely Seat

Great Shunner Fell

My Best Route *(from Hardraw, near Hawes)*

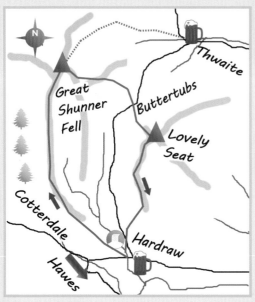

1.   Climbing Great Shunner Fell from Hardraw is straightforward, the Pennine Way is clearly marked, obvious on the ground and leads directly to the summit. The crossing to Lovely Seat is also not difficult to follow thanks to a convenient fence. From the summit of Lovely Seat there is a choice; either take on the peat hags on a direct descent over the shoulder of Lovely Seat or, particularly in bad/wet weather, return to the road at Buttertubs.

2.   From Hardraw take the Pennine Way path bordered by stone walls that leaves the road just to the west of the Green Dragon pub. After 1km the lane becomes more open and the track winds its way steadily NW. From the gate (shown on the photo on p57) the path turns north, with some paved sections and leads direct to the summit of Great Shunner Fell.

3.   From Great Shunner Fell follow the fence for 2km ESE then turn SSE for 500m to the high point of the road (known as Buttertubs). Cross the road to the south of the cattle grid and head alongside the fence (initially boggy but improving) which carries on up Lovely Seat.

4.   After spending five minutes in the summit 'seat' head south and then SSW over trackless land. The views compensate for the rough terrain which continues to Pike Hill and a bridleway. Follow the track down to the road and enter the hamlet of High Shaw. Rather than keep to the road, a footpath cuts across fields to Hardraw just before Simonstone Hall.

5.   A return to Hawes adds 1.5m each way. A footpath leaves Hardraw to the south and cuts ESE to the road leading into the market town.

Green Dragon pub

Great Shunner Fell

Great Shunner Fell

Buttertubs

Buttertubs is the high road pass between Hawes and Thwaite in Upper Swaledale. It is interesting for walkers but fascinating for both cyclists and those in a car.

Jeremy Clarkson once described the road on either side of the pass as "England's only truly spectacular road". For cyclists it provided the most spectacular scenes from the Grand Depart on the Tour de France, the breathtaking overhead shots showcasing the lovely Dales landscape in all its glory.

For the mere walker though it is simply the crossing between the two high fells of Great Shunner Fell and Lovely Seat.

The name Buttertubs comes from the limestone potholes formed in the rock face. Legend has it that the holes were used by farmers to store their butter on the way to market...maybe.

Anyway it's a good name and a great spot.

Alternative Route (From Thwaite) 15.5km/9.5 miles

Head NW from the village centre and take the lane heading west marked Great Shunner Fell. This is the Pennine Way. At a stone barn turn uphill and pass through a gate and two stiles. The route is now climbing quite steeply but is easy to follow to the summit of Great Shunner Fell.

The crossing to Lovely Seat is not as bad as many have stated (except the wet peat just to the east of the road). From Great Shunner the route (barely a path so follow the fence all the way to Little Seat via Buttertubs), goes SSE then south to the col. The climb to Lovely Seat is boggy initially but improves. Return to the col, the land north of Lovely Seat is very rough. From Buttertubs walk down the road into Thwaite, great views and the most scenic part of the route taken in the Tour de France.

Many 'tick' these two mountains with a quick up and down from Buttertubs pass.

Dodd Fell Hill

2,192ft (668m)

Wether Fell 2,014ft (614m)

Key Details (My Best Route)

Distance:	17km (10.5 miles)
Height to Climb:	580m (1,900ft)
O/S Explorer Map:	OL30 Yorkshire Dales North & Central
Parking:	SD 872893 Gayle. just east of the bridge, Road Side.

Gayle Mill

My View

To the north of Hawes lies the pair of Great Shunner Fell and Lovely Seat. Similarly paired but lying to the south is the more enjoyable circuit of Dodd Fell Hill and Wether Fell (the summit area is known as Drumaldrace). Circling the valley of Sleddale, this horseshoe is full of interest throughout and enjoys outstanding views in all directions, but most particularly over the Three Peaks to the south.

Most of the walking is on excellent tracks enabling the walk to pass quicker than the mileage would suggest. The exceptions to this are the short climbs to the summit. These are trackless and more the home of grouse beaters than walkers. Any tracks that are near the two summits are of limited use so stick to a compass bearing, knowing that the pleasure of leaping from peat hag to peat hag is only for a limited time.

As the tracks are good my mind tends to wander more than usual. This is an area steeped in history and present day economics, a microcosm of the Dales. History can be found on the Roman Road, on the water powered cotton mills, stone settlements and the old trig point on Dodd Fell Hill. Today's land use is set all around; from sheep farming to grouse shooting, tourism in the form of the Wensleydale Creamery and Gayle Mill to one of the largest forestry plantations in the area, it is a working landscape. Keep alert and open your eyes to the landscape on this excellent walk....unless the cloud is down!

Looking east from Wether Fell

Dodd Fell Hill

My Best Route

(from Gayle, near Hawes)

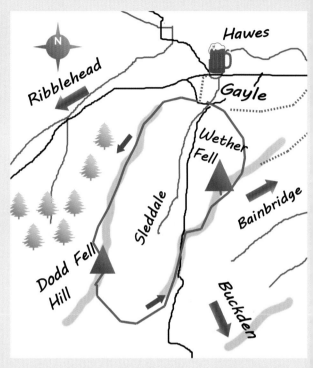

1.   Head for the western extremity of the village of Gayle and take the clearly marked Pennine Way WSW, initially via a well protected lane but soon into open countryside. The path/track climbs steadily for over 2.5km turning SSW before the land flattens out at the 'inspirational' name of Ten End Peat Ground. After a further 1km leave the track and head uphill. The final 100m climb is on tussocky ground to the summit trig point of Dodd Fell Hill. The trig point is not the highest point but the driest (sensible lads these surveyors).

2.   From the summit of Dodd Fell Hill go south for 200m then turn SSE for 750km and join the Cam High Road. Heading due east (the shortest route) is purgatory. The Cam High Road is one of those arrow straight roads much beloved by the Romans. It makes for quick walking and aside from one short stretch of real road, the main danger comes from off road vehicles and forestry lorries. However, both are rare and it is peaceful countryside.

3.   As the track climbs towards Wether Fell (from point 541m) the main decision is when to cut off and head for the summit. The best place is 150m beyond a wall at point 586m. The bridleway heading west at this point does not help in finding the summit, in fact it circles the highest land. A trackless 25m climb brings you to a small cairn with good views (named Drumaldrace). Although there is a path heading NE from here it is for a set of grouse butts which pepper the area, sensible walkers return SE to the Cam Road.

4.   Back on the track carry on for 750m. When a wall is reached, pass through and take the bridleway heading north. Pass through two gates and make a short steep descent, all on a good path. The track continues north but there is a gate on your left, soon after you meet a wall. Take this footpath and follow it down through numerous fields of sheep and stiles as it drops quite steeply into Gayle.

Dodd Fell Hill

Pennine Way near Dodd Fell Hill

Alternative Routes

Wether Fell itself has a few pleasant options to make a shorter day from Wensleydale but these are not easily combined with Dodd Fell Hill.

(From Gayle or Burtersett)

A circular walk which combines these two villages can include a climb of Wether Fell. Start from Burtersett on the bridleway which climbs steadily up Wether Fell and then vary the return by taking the footpath to Gayle. Before reaching Gayle a footpath tracks east along the hillside back to Burtersett.

(From Bainbridge)

A longer but easy route from Bainbridge follows the Cam High Road all the way to Wether Fell. Vary the return by taking the bridleway to Countersett near Semer Water.

Dodd Fell Hill is not easily accessed from anywhere except Hawes.

Gayle Mill

The waters of Gayle Beck flow swiftly down Sleddale before arriving in the pretty village of Gayle. Here a beautifully preserved mill is an excellent example of how a water powered cotton mill worked in the past, in an era when industry, not tourism, dominated.

The wooden water wheel is just one of a number of features that brings history alive. It is well worth a visit.

Follow the river a few metres further and reach the Wensleydale Creamery, world famous for its excellent cheeses.

How Many Dales?

There are 40 dales in the Yorkshire Dales. Many of these though are short and feed off the six main dales: Wharfedale, Ribblesdale, Dentdale, Garsdale, Wensleydale and Swaledale.

Wharfedale is the longest of the dales; 70 miles from Cam Fell to Cawood where it joins the Ouse.

Nidderdale is often described as one of the main dales but lies outside the National Park in an Area of Outstanding Natural Beauty.

Settle to Carlisle Railway

Taking a ride on the highly acclaimed Settle to Carlisle railway not only offers the passenger great views but is a wonderful stopping off point to climb many of the Dales 30. Mark Corner of the Yorkshire Dales Society has led many walks from these isolated stations...

Ribblehead

Construction of this scenic railway line began in 1869. Built largely by hand, with up to 6,000 men working on it at its peak, its many highlights include the iconic Ribblehead viaduct. The line was threatened with closure in 1983 but a campaign to save it, supported by many lovers of the Dales, was ultimately successful in 1989. As well as the regular mainline services, weekly steam charters grace the line in the summer months.

By letting the train take the strain you can be in the Dales from Leeds or Carlisle in just over an hour. The stations at Horton, Ribblehead, Dent, Garsdale and Kirkby Stephen provide ideal starting points for a hill bagging circular walk or you can enjoy a linear walk from station to station (my favourite).

Horton in Ribblesdale is perfect for climbing Fountains Fell or the impressive Pen-y-Ghent (my favourite of the 'Three Peaks' and one which our family climb each Boxing Day before turkey soup!). Horton is also the traditional launch pad for the demanding "Three Peaks Challenge" of Pen-y-Ghent, Whernside and Ingleborough. Ribblehead Station, by the stunning viaduct, gives easy access to Whernside and Ingleborough or to Gragareth and Dodd Fell for a longer trek. Before your return train a fine selection of ales is available at the welcoming Station Inn!

Dentdale is one of my favourite dales and the charming station at Dent is a fine starting point for Whernside or for conquering Great Knoutberry Hill or Great Coum.

Note though that the station, the highest mainline one in England, is several miles from the fine village of Dent (it's a long way for an after walk pint).

The final section of the line through the Dales goes from Garsdale Station to Kirkby Stephen Station passing through Mallerstang, originally part of Westmorland, now Cumbria, but part of the Yorkshire Dales National Park.

Some of the best scenery and walking in the Dales is to be found here, including the Dales 30 summits of Wild Boar Fell, Swarth Fell, Little Fell and High Seat. I would strongly recommend the tough but exhilarating walk from Kirkby Stephen Station (again a fair way out of town) to Garsdale Station via Wild Boar Fell, including a celebratory pint at the Moorcock Inn (this is the Best Route described on page 36). The views from the tops are breathtaking. The vista of the Howgills to the west is one of my favourites and whets the appetite to explore its peaks.

So, leave the car at home and use public transport to explore this very special area. You can look out of the window of your bus or train on your return journey and admire with a sense of satisfaction the ground you've covered.

If you do not want to plan and tackle the walks from these spectacular stations on your own then join a group organised by the Friends of the Settle to Carlisle line. You are also very welcome to join walks in the Dales with the Yorkshire Dales Society, most of which are accessible from public transport including the DalesBus as well as the rail line.

Wild Boar Fell

Upper Wharfedale

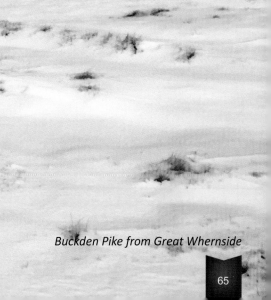

The head of Wharfedale is ringed by a number of attractive fells. Long broad ridges offer miles of upland walking. The effort of climbing the steep lower slopes is compensated by the rewards of the summit ridges. Each fell is different though, some will be more memorable than others.
There are four 'Dales 30'summits in Upper Wharfedale.

Buckden Pike from Great Whernside

Great Whernside 2,310ft (704m)

Litton

My View

Great Whernside holds much in common with its more illustrious, certainly more popular (and oddly higher) namesake to the west. They are both large whaleback mountains, boggy and hard going on their flanks, and end in a broad flat summit ridge where the ground hardly rises or falls for hundreds of metres. Great Whernside does however boast an interesting assembly of millstone grit boulders on the summit, a great place to linger and enjoy the excellent views over Upper Wharfedale.

Apparently it is possible to see the coast on each side of the country but despite others claiming this distinction, I have never observed even one! Neither have I seen the ghost at Hag Dyke youth hostel or the lost souls on the Fellsman challenge (apparently some are still up there) but what I have done is climb in all four seasons and all extremes of weather. My only tip is that the bog to the south is just that, boggy.

I have always enjoyed my visits to Great Whernside, the peace and tranquillity particularly appealing after my more regular visits to the more popular fells in the west. It is a proper mountain and the easy walking on the summit ridge offers the walker a chance to completely relax, take in the 360 degree views and not have to bother avoiding hearty groups of multi-coloured walkers – the lapwings will do fine, or even a buzzard.

Summit of Great Whernside

Great Whernside

My Best Route *(from Kettlewell)*

1. Until 1997 there were no public rights of way up Great Whernside but there are now (which is a relief as it significantly eases progress to the summit). This route is the quickest and most direct way to the top and offers a pleasant if longer descent.

2. Leave the village heading due east, cross the river at its east end and from the lane look almost immediately for a sign for Hag Dyke and Providence Pot. The climb starts here and winds steadily up the hillside to the buildings at Hag Dyke. Hag Dyke is a youth hostel run by the Ben Rhydding Scout Group and includes the highest chapel in England. From the hostel a steep climb heading ENE, a flatter section, then a final steep climb brings you to the summit boulder field. A trig point and enormous cairn adorn the summit.

3. Head north from the summit for 750m to a derelict shelter (part of the old industrial works) where a path leaves the ridge heading NNW. For the best views however, walk a little further along the ridge before cutting west at a stile to join the path. The path skirts the fellside before dropping sharply (and often wetly) NW to the Kettlewell/Coverdale road.

4. Cross the road and follow the lower wall as it winds westwards along the lower slopes of Buckden Pike. The route to Buckden Pike heads along a path WNW from 100m up the road. Keep to the wall though if not climbing Buckden Pike.

5. Follow the wall for 1.5km initially west but gradually turning SW. As the path turns SW it divides. Head south on the left hand fork. From here the going is straightforward and leads directly into Kettlewell, the path turning into a rough landrover track (Top Mere Road) half way down. The views over Kettlewell are good.

Kettlewell

Great Whernside

Great Whernside from the West

Wharfedale Three Peaks

Hundreds if not thousands of walkers take to the fells of the Yorkshire Three Peaks (Pen-y-Ghent, Whernside and Ingleborough) every Saturday during the summer months. This creates environmental problems on and near the paths but can also turn into a tedious (and very long) route march where you are surrounded by crowds of people.

One of the solutions is the development of a WHARFEDALE THREE PEAKS CHALLENGE as an alternative.

Great Whernside 2,310ft

Buckden Pike 2,303ft

Birks 2,000ft

This covers 18 miles in total and over 4,000ft of climbing.

Starting and finishing at the pretty village of Kettlewell the challenge may not be as long, but is certainly as tough as the popular Yorkshire Three Peaks. The terrain is rougher and the paths not as manicured. It is an excellent alternative.

The route can be extended from Buckden Pike with a visit to Cray. For full details visit the Where2walk website.

Alternative Routes

(Kettlewell heading south initially)

Leaving Kettlewell follow the minor road south along the east side of the River Wharfe for 1.5km. Turn left on a farm track as it passes through a copse before emerging on the open mountainside. Head directly up hill; the going is good till you reach a wall at a height of 500m. From the wall the peat hags make for hard going but persevere and once the final summit slopes are met it is a pleasant tramp along the broad ridge. Return via the ascent or descent of the Best Route.

(From the East)

The route from the reservoirs of Nidderdale is trackless and boggy, not overly appealing.

Buckden Pike

2,303ft (702m)

Key Details (My Best Route)

Distance:	9km (5.5 miles)
Height to Climb:	460m (1,510ft)
O/S Explorer Map:	OL30 Yorkshire Dales North & Central
Parking:	SD 942773 Buckden, Car Park.

Polish Memorial

My View

Upper Wharfedale is one of my favourite areas of the Dales. The mountains themselves all have their own personality and they are complemented by some of the most attractive villages and scenery around. It is the image of the Dales. From Upper Wharfedale the four mountains offer an imposing backdrop, ringing the valley head as impressively as many a Lakeland valley.

Buckden Pike is the best, a proper mountain which can compete happily with the better known Three Peaks further west. It should attract many more visitors.

The Polish War Memorial and cairn with trig point bookmark the wide and enjoyable mile long summit ridge. From here the views are outstanding, the newly laid path ensuring that the view can be enjoyed without needing to concentrate on leaping from one peat hag to another.

On my last visit I explored the lead mines at the top of Buckden Beck, something I had contrived to miss in the past. Past the mines the route down took me to a wall only 100m above the village of Buckden with surely one of the best views in all England. The Yorkshire stone village of Buckden is in the foreground, lonely Langstrothdale lies between Yockenthwaite Moor and Birks and to the right limestone cliffs complete a perfectly framed view.

Summit of Buckden Pike looking west

Buckden Pike

My Best Route
(from Buckden)

1.   A bridleway leaves the large car park in Buckden and heads NNW up the side of the fell. Having passed through some woodland the track enters open countryside, turns NNE and reaches a wall. The path divides with a signpost pointing uphill to Buckden Pike. From here the path gradually climbs NE (through three gates) for 1.5km before reaching a wall. Turn SE and climb steeply beside the wall to the summit. There are fine views from here although quite why there is a large wooden pole next to the cairn is a matter of conjecture.

2.   An easy and recently restored path leads along the west side of a wall for 1km to a large cross dedicated to Polish airman lost on a training exercise in 1942. It is well worth a visit. From here return towards the summit until the path meets a wall just to its south. Turn west on the south side of the wall and head downhill.

3.   The path turns SW and then SSW to the old lead mine workings at the top of Buckden Gill at 650m. From here cross the small bridge and follow a marked bridleway that skirts the fellside for 1km heading SSW. Where the wall turns steeply downhill

Summit of Buckden Pike

towards Buckden, follow it, aiming directly for the village. When a wall blocks your progress follow the wall to the right for 40m to a gate. A path leads back to the car park.

4.   **Descent Options**: From the lead mines a track does lead directly down the gill but it is rough and little fun. A more attractive option is to leave the path 200m short of the mines and follow the footpath west until it meets the uphill route at 941784.

Buckden Pike

Summit plateau of Buckden Pike

Dry Stone Walls

There are more than 5,000 miles of dry stone walls in the Yorkshire Dales.

They are called dry stone walls because they are built without mortar, their own structure ensuring they stay upright. They are built using larger stones at the base (the base can be double the width of the top of the wall), filled with smaller ones for stability and capped by a 'crown' stone at the top.

Mainly built in the last 500 years the walls were used to contain animals (usually sheep) or crops. Many are now falling into disrepair but they still are one of the main features of the landscape.

Polish War Memorial

The Polish War Memorial is dedicated to the six Polish air crew who crashed on Buckden Pike in January 1942 on a training flight. Five died immediately but 'Jo' the tail gunner crawled (literally) through a blizzard to the pub at Cray. He survived and in 1972 built the memorial in memory of his dead colleagues.

Parts of the aircraft are embedded into the base of the memorial.

Alternative Routes

(From the East)

A bridleway at the road end of the Walden Valley leads west to within a few hundred metres of the summit of Buckden Pike. At this point (964788) take a direct ascent west to the trig point. The bridleway, although intermittent at times, offers an unusual route to the summit. From the summit walk south to the Polish War Memorial and carry on SE following the wall for 200m. However, at the gate turn sharp NE and rejoin the bridleway which leads back to the Walden Valley.

(From the South)

A long route heads north from Kettlewell all the way to the summit of Buckden Pike (6.5km distant) initially up Top Mere track and then onto the long south shoulder of Buckden Pike. This is part of the Bracken Way, an excellent new long distance footpath in the Yorkshire Dales.

Yockenthwaite Moor 2,110ft (643m)

Stalling Busk

Key Details (My Best Route)

Distance:	15km (9.5 miles)
Height to Climb:	420m (1,378ft)
O/S Explorer Map:	OL30 Yorkshire Dales North & Central
Parking:	SD 903862 Marsett, Raydale. Off Road

My View

Yockenthwaite Moor is one of the Dales 30 mountains which makes this a 'proper' challenge. There are many excellent fells in the Dales 30 but even its most ardent admirer would not say Yockenthwaite Moor is one of them. A large expanse of peat bog of between two and three kilometres wide marks the boundary of Wharfedale and Wensleydale, the river of peat stretching for many kilometres west of the summit, legend saying that it becomes even less pleasant before it reaches the Pennine Way.

I have only once come across a worse approach to a summit (further north on Mickle Fell) certainly nothing in the Lakes or Scotland can compete.

In an attempt to be positive, I would say that any approach from the north has some excellent access/tracks up to the plateau; Raydale and Semer Water are both very pleasant places to visit and I am led to believe the views are good (my three visits were shrouded in cloud despite promising weather forecasts).

The other benefit of approaching from the north is that there is a convenient fence which helps what could be a very difficult navigational challenge. The fence leads to the summit and back down to the track back to Raydale.

I can only add that on my crossing I actually lost a boot in the squelch, I had to dig it out from well over a foot down. Maybe best to tackle Yockenthwaite Moor when the ground is frozen and not just pretending to be...

Yockenthwaite Moor

Yockenthwaite Moor

My Best Route

(from Marsett, Raydale)

1. I parked in Marsett, crossed to the south bank of the tributary stream and headed east to cross the main river out of Semer Water. Climb steeply into Stalling Busk.

2. From Stalling Busk head a few metres north on the road then join a footpath climbing steeply south to the old drovers track linking Wensleydale and Upper Wharfedale. Follow the track for 3.5km of quick walking. At a sharp 45 degree bend and gate leave the track and follow a wall turning into a fence heading SW.

3. The first 1km is straightforward on good turf. As the fence gradually bends towards the west the terrain deteriorates into peat hags. Keep the fence in sight and pick the best route, there is no path. There are two new fences coming in at right angles, do not follow these (check your compass) and head west to the summit trig point.

4. From the trig point follow the fence, which turns into a wall, north for a further 1km over the peat hags. After 1km there is a gate in a wall running at right angles, this is the start of shooting country. From here carry on north past some shooting butts to another wall after 750m. Follow the wall NE to an obvious access road. This road leads downhill, past some forestry on the left, to Raydale House.

5. Take the main access road to the farm and follow it for 1.5km back to Marsett.

6. For a memorable day it is possible to park at the NE end of Semer Water and include a pleasant circuit of the lake in the walk.

Yockenthwaite Moor

Summit Trig Point

Alternative Routes

From Wharfedale.

The quickest way to access Yockenthwaite Moor is direct from Yockenthwaite itself. Climb steeply for 330m to the plateau. Head north for nearly 1km to the trig point. In cloud the trig may be difficult to locate as the plateau is nearly flat. If you hit a fence turn left and follow it to the summit. If you veer to the west of the trig point there is no clue to where you are. Either aim off to the east of north to strike the fence or take a GPS to locate the summit.

Other options from Wharfedale are possible. The ascents from Cray/ Hubberholme are not very pleasant.

Peat Hags

Peat is an organic soil that forms in cold, acidic, waterlogged conditions. Mosses and plants such as sphagnum grow and die creating the thick layers of peat. Bronze Age deforestation helped accelerate the process of what became known as a blanket bog on our upland areas.

Peat itself is good for the environment with its high carbon content and its capacity to absorb and hold water reducing flooding on low-lands. However, much of our peat has been used as drainage, grazing and moorland burning creating a drier peat that breaks down creating the unpleasant peat bogs which form much of the Pennine spine of the country.

The flatness of some of the high moorland accelerates this breakdown and creates the 'rivers' of peat so disliked by walkers.

Semer Water

The second largest natural lake in the Yorkshire Dales (there are very few due to the porous nature of the bedrock) is 800m long, has a nature reserve to its south and attracts fishermen, water sport enthusiasts and nature lovers alike.

If you time your visit to Semer Water in July you may be rewarded with one of the finest displays of yellow water lillies, often described as upturned brandy bottles, settling on the lakes surface.

Birks Fell

2,003ft (610m)

My View

I have a sneaking affection for Birks, the long wide ridge is a perfect place to stride out and enjoy the vast landscape of the central Dales. It is at its best on frozen ground in the winter months but I have never encountered unpleasant terrain underfoot at any time of the year.

So few people venture to its summit that the main difficulty is not the over eroded paths of the nearby Three Peaks but actually finding and following them.

Most of the paths are 'through' routes from Wharfedale to Littondale with Birks itself an irrelevent bystander. One of these routes passes close to the trig point but beware, this is not the highest point which is over a mile away. The real summit has no public footpaths anywhere near it.

Birks forms a graceful (but long) spur between Upper Wharfedale to the east and Littondale to the south west with Langstrothdale forming the northern barrier.

The vast shoulder of Birks stretches north past a tarn to the summit before bending west, over the trig point at Horse Head until it eventually drops into Ribblesdale north of Pen-y-Ghent, so uniform in height that Horse Head was until recently deemed the highest point. The entire ridge is over 12 miles long.

Upper Wharfedale from Birks

Birks Fell

My Best Route *(from Kettlewell)*

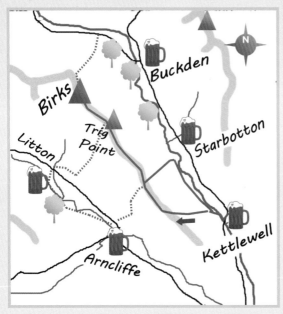

1.   Birks can be similarly climbed from both Kettlewell in Wharfedale or Arncliffe in Littondale. I prefer the Kettlewell route as I like a choice of pubs at the end of the day!

2.   From the car park at Kettlewell turn right, cross the road bridge, then immediately turn right off the road and head NNW. A farm track passes a gate within 100m and a footpath leaves the track to the left and heads steeply west up hill. It passes through a classic limestone scar which involves a little bit of scrambling. It's a good spot. From here the path climbs steeply to the shoulder of Birks at 480m.

3.   There is a wall along the summit ridge of Birks which will accompany the walker from here to the summit. It is a solid wall which can only be crossed at a right of way. Stick to the east side of the wall until it drops sharply to the right after 250m. A stile passes over the wall to the left and then meets a further wall heading NW to the trig point.

4.   Three metres higher and nearly 2km along the ridge is a small insignificant cairn on the other side of the wall, this is the highest point of Birks. Return to the main trig point, a return enlivened by Birks Tarn and the ruins of an old building built into the wall. With the red grouse squawking and the skylark circling it is a pleasant part of the day.

5.   The best option from the trig point is to follow the outbound route to point 944730 at 520m where a bridleway from Arncliffe crosses the shoulder of Birks. Turn ENE and descend until the bridleway splits above steep slopes. Turn SE towards Kettlewell along a farm track which keeps above the scar before zig zagging down the steeper section into Kettlewell.

Kettlewell

Birks Fell

The route to the 'highest point'

Alternative Route (From Litton)

 The quickest way to climb Birks is from Litton in Littondale. A bridleway leads NE directly to the trig point, then drops down near to Buckden. The highest point of Birks is nearly 2km to the NW of the trig point.

An alternative descent follows the ridge SE from the trig point (not the summit) and picks up the track heading SW directly to Arncliffe in Littondale at the 520m contour. Return to Litton along the River Skirfare.

(From Hubberholme)

A more direct assault to the highest point/summit can be made from the hamlet of Hubberholme but this is over rough ground and is a relentless grind.

U Shaped Valleys

On either side of Birks lie two perfectly formed U shaped glacial valleys, Wharfedale and Littondale. They represent a geographer's dream and are two of the best examples in the country. The valleys were formed in the Devensian period roughly 80,000 years ago.

It is particularly noteworthy how dead straight the valleys are, only serious mountain massifs such as Buckden Pike, to the east of Birks causing any significant change of direction and even these have struggled to resist the ices power.

Calendar Girls and Kettlewell

Although this successful 2003 film was about the Rylstone Women's Institute most of the filming was done in and around Kettlewell.

Other reasons to visit this lovely Dales village are the very popular Scarecrow Festival which is in mid August (a must for families) and the fine array of local, cottage style businesses.

The Smithy has a particularly fine choice of paintings and photography from local artists.

Fixing the fells

Matt Neale is one of the most experienced rangers in the Yorkshire Dales National Park, operating mainly in the north of the region. The job of a ranger is varied, interesting and not without its challenges.

You will find rangers working in National Parks and protected landscapes all around the world. Here in the Yorkshire Dales National Park, where the majority of the land is privately owned, they play a key role in linking the local community, visitors and the National Park Authority. The Ranger Service offers technical advice and support through three area based teams.

Within these teams the rangers offer hands-on support and advice to farmers, land managers, parish councils, local groups, visitors and individuals. If the Rangers can't help directly, they will usually know someone who can!

The Ranger Service plays a major part in providing opportunities for both local people and visitors to enjoy the special qualities of the National Park. We maintain 1600 miles of public footpaths, bridleways and byways, which provide a superb way of getting out and about. Although the local topography can be challenging, we carry out additional works in certain areas to enable access for those with limited mobility. There are also iconic National Trails to maintain, such as the Pennine Way as well as other classic routes such as the Three Yorkshire Peaks, Dales Way and the Coast to Coast walk.

We work closely with landowners to construct and repair 'infrastructure' that you will find along a public right of way. Stiles, gates, fingerposts, bridges, surface repairs are all the type of works that we undertake.

All stiles and gates on public rights of way are actually the legal responsibility of the landowner. The Yorkshire Dales National Park Authority usually offers 100% grant aid to landowners towards the upkeep of most of these items. That generally means that we will provide the necessary materials and labour to ensure that these features are in good condition and usable by the public.

A Ranger's Life

Where possible, we will try and improve access features so those with limited mobility can also enjoy the countryside more easily. Replacing a ladder stile with a kissing gate might sound straightforward enough, but there is a lot of negotiation to be done with the landowner first. Gates can get left open, there is a gap to be made in a dry stone wall, and occasionally sheep can squeeze through standard kissing gates.

We have developed a range of tips and tricks over the years to reduce perceived problems – to help persuade landowners that a gate can often be an improvement over a stile.

Of course, the dry stone walls are important heritage features, and in some cases have been standing for many hundreds of years. Some of the gap stiles through the walls are equally important as heritage features and some examples are definitely worthy of conservation, so not all stiles are necessarily up for conversion to gates.

One 'first world' problem we occasionally encounter is pet dogs stuck in stone squeeze stiles. Usually the animals appear to be overweight and the action of them trying to get through a tight gap and then crouching means they get jammed. Often this involves a dismantling and time consuming stile rebuild; it's all part of a day's work!...

I have been fortunate to meet some interesting characters through my work. I have accompanied some well known folks on visits to the National Park, such as John Prescott when he was deputy Prime Minister, who I marched up a steep-ish hill whilst talking about public footpaths and their 'value'. He was a bit short of breath, so I had the opportunity to do most of the chatting!

To find out more about the rangers please visit the National Park website.

Western Dales

Ingleborough from Twisleton Scar

The Western Dales display the most dramatic landscape in the area. Showcased by the lovely limestone scars and pavements the area has excellent walking and challenging summits. The Three Peaks are extremely popular but climb the other peaks for a totally different experience. Both options are good.
There are ten 'Dales 30' summits in the Western Dales.

Fountains Fell

2,192ft 668m)

Darnbrook Fell 2,047ft (624m)

Old Coke Oven

My View

It's a strange thing. Fountains Fell (and by default Darnbrook Fell) have a reputation of dreary monotony. Read the various descriptions of people climbing the mountains and it is usually in poor conditions, often with snow on the ground and rarely with any pleasure. On my last visit I watched a group of 20 Pennine Way walkers fail to venture off the Way to visit Fountains Fell's fascinating and historic summit area. Rarely visited, rarely loved and mainly unfair.

My climbs were also done in moderate weather, blighted by stationary cloud which never moved; neighbouring Pen-y-Ghent, Littondale and Malham all bathed in autumn sunshine. Albeit frustrating from a photography perspective the weather did not stop me enjoying these two fells. In particular the easy climb of Fountains Fell and exploration of the summit is a genuine highlight.

On bleaker Darnbrook there is intrigue; the O/S trig point stands high and dry on an exposed lump of peat, exposing its massive base of concrete used in the early 20th Century to anchor it (they took some constructing). It is not even on the highest point, just a convenient lump of peat. Coming off Darnbrook is challenging (the tussocks surely as high as anywhere in the Dales) but once on a hump there is a satisfaction of some excellent views down lovely Littondale.

Fountains Fell is named after Fountains Abbey and the Cistercian Monks who used to walk the area, now that is fascinating!

Pen-y-Ghent from the summit of Fountains Fell

Fountains Fell

My Best Route *(from Tennant Gill Farm, nr Malham)*

1.	Park on the Malham to Arncliffe roadside near Tennant Gill Farm. Pass through the gate of the farm. The path follows the well-trodden Pennine Way (sign posted) and heads directly up Fountains Fell. It is straightforward to follow and easy to walk. The Pennine Way does not visit the summit of Fountains Fell, which is to the south west of the Way's high point and 4km from the start. Just before arriving at some tall boy cairns (and after

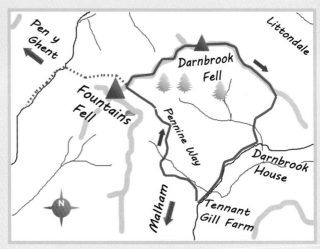

the warning on mine shafts) take the faint track south west for 500m to the summit cairn.

2.	Return to the Pennine Way and continue NW for 100m to a gate in a wall. Before the gate take the faint track NE. Keep close to the wall as it bends right after 200m and after a further 200m climb over a locked gate. The faint track continues alongside the wall (now on your right) for a further 250m. At this point the wall has collapsed and two planks of wood cover the gap. Cross over here and then carry on following the wall NE which is now on your left. After 1km a fence appears, follow this SE for 300m to Darnbrook Fell's summit.

3.	The trig point (intriguingly exposing its massive concrete base) is not the highest point so there is no need to try and cross the fence. The high point is a few metres to the south. Pick your own block of peat.

4.	The descent involves either a return to the Pennine Way (quickest) or the completion of a circular walk arriving at the road at Darnbrook House (preferred). To achieve the latter follow the fence, soon becoming a wall that heads initially east before bending in a SE direction. There is a faint track next to the wall but when the wall disappears east carry on south over very tussocky and awkward terrain. This is trackless. Heading south now the land drops steeply to meet the river NW of Darnbrook House. A track leads to the farm and the Malham Tarn to Arncliffe road.

It is a 2km walk back to the start.

Fountains Fell

Darnbrook Fell

Alternative Routes

(From the West)

Similar to the Best Route this makes use of the easy access to Fountains Fell via the Pennine Way. Starting at a cattle grid 1.5km NE of Dale Head Farm follow the path east to Fountains Fell. Make the crossing as described opposite to Darnbrook Fell before reversing the route all the way back to Dale Head Farm.

It is possible to include the route from the NW with the two Dales 30 peaks to the north, Pen-y-Ghent and Plovers Hill using Dale Head Farm as the base.

Mining on Fountains Fell

The summit of Fountains Fell is pot marked with numerous deep mine shafts. These are the remnants of coke mining in the 19th Century; coke being lighter and easier to transport than coal.

An old coke oven is still standing (built in 1807 by Lord Ribblesdale) amongst the mine shafts on the summit plateau. The coke was transported down to the lead smelting works on Malham Moor.

The oven itself is built of roughly coursed sandstone rubble and measures about 4m square and 2m at its highest. Inside, the oven consists of a hemispherical dome (giving it the name of a beehive oven) though now the top has collapsed.

Mining was carried out on Fountains Fell for well over 30 years.

Malham Tarn

Malham Tarn is England's highest freshwater lake at 377m (1,237ft).

It is classed as a lake not a tarn (there are many higher tarns) as the water area formed naturally after the glacial period as opposed to being scoured out by a mountain glacier. Tarns are often much deeper than lakes although this is rarely the case in the Dales.

The only other natural lake in the Dales is Semer Water in Wensleydale.

Pen-y-Ghent 2,277ft (694m)

Plover Hill 2,231ft (680m)

Key Details (My Best Route)

Distance:	12km (7.5 miles)
Height to Climb:	540m (1,775ft)
O/S Explorer Map:	OL2 Yorkshire Dales South & West
Parking:	SD 808726 .Horton in Ribblesdale, Car Park.

My View

A proper little mountain. Shapely and isolated from its neighbours Pen-y-Ghent provides an inspiring outline from any direction, particularly when approaching Horton in Ribblesdale from Settle. I always enjoy it, it is an easy day (or half day) when it is climbed on its own, whilst for those on the Three Peaks challenge it is an encouraging start to a long day.

Pen-y-Ghent is in fact a one mile wide ridge with the rarely visited Plover Hill marking the northern end. The views from Plover Hill are even better than Pen-y-Ghent with an excellent perspective of the Three Peaks and good views into lovely Littondale. Regardless of any desire to tick the summit it is worth the extra effort to visit the cairn.

I was on Plovers when someone asked me if my dog was enjoying herself; I paused, thought about it and said I'd never asked her.

It is unusual in the Dales for a climb to include any kind of rock scrambling but Pen-y-Ghent does. After joining the Pennine Way at the well known 'hole in the wall' the climb is steep, rocky with a couple of places where the use of hands becomes helpful. The children love it and so does the child in the rest of us!

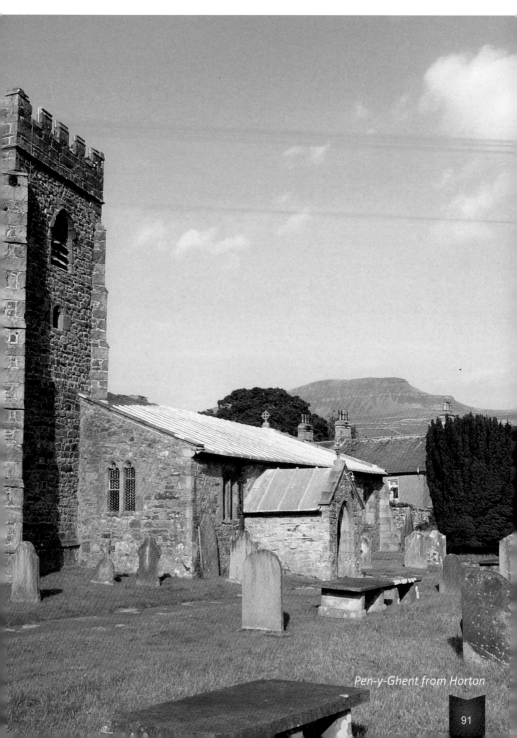

Pen-y-Ghent from Horton

Pen-y-Ghent

My Best Route *(from Horton in Ribblesdale)*

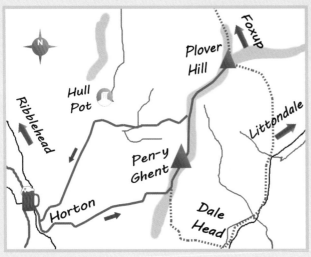

1. From the car park walk south along the road to the church. Take the track alongside the graveyard, cross the river, pass the school and head along the lane to Bracken Bottom Farm.

2. From the gate just before the farm at Bracken Bottom, the path climbs steadily through undulating terrain and limestone outcrops for 2km before arriving at the 'Hole in the Wall'. The path now joins the Pennine Way. The climb north from here to the summit is steep and rocky but with no great gremlins. There is one point where hands are definitely helpful but the summit plateau is soon reached. A further 200m brings the trig point, cairn and comfortable wind break with seating.

3. The summit plateau/ridge stretches for 2km to Plover Hill. The main path crosses the wall at the summit but for Plover Hill keep to the west of the wall and head north for 1km to the col. The path then bends in a north easterly direction to the small summit cairn of Plovers.

4. Return SW and then south to the col. From here head west and marginally downhill meeting the main track off Pen-y-Ghent after 200m. Head west for 1.5km along an excellent, recently built path (managed by the Three Peaks Society) to a meeting of paths near Hull Pot.

5. There is a junction of paths in a small hollow. The intrepid Three Peakers head up hill in a westerly direction, those wanting a short visit to Hull Pot will head NNE for 200m whilst the route back to Horton joins a farm track heading SSW. In 2km the track reaches the village of Horton, opposite the Pen-y-Ghent Cafe.

Hole in the Wall

Pen-y-Ghent

Pen-y-Ghent from Ribblehead.

Alternative Routes

(From the East)

A track leads WNW then NNE from Dale Head Farm on the Stainforth to Halton Gill (Littondale) minor road. It joins the Best Route at the Hole in the Wall before carrying on to the summit.

Follow the broad shoulder north to Plover Hill then pick a route ESE (trackless) from here down the hillside to meet the road roughly 3km north of Dale Head Farm. There are no walls on this part of the descent.

(From the North)

An interesting route up Plover Hill starts from Foxup near Halton Gill. Follow the Pennine Journey track west for 2.5km then turn south for a short sharp climb to Plover Hill. This avoids the scramble on the south shoulder of Pen-y-Ghent.

An alternative (scramble avoiding) route is to reverse the descent from Horton on the Best Route. The path is in superb condition and easy all the way up.

Hull Pot

Just to the north of the Pennine Way/Three Peaks main descent of Pen-y-Ghent lies the collapsed cavern of Hull Pot, the largest natural hole in England ... apparently. It is nearly 100m long and 18m wide, an impressive sight whatever the weather.

It is at its best after heavy rains when a waterfall cascades into the cavern and then disappears underground, to emerge near the village of Horton. There are stories of the hole filling with water creating its own lake after a particularly heavy spell of rain.

Shake Holes

One of commonest questions I am asked when undertaking a map reading course is what is a 'shake hole'

They are formed where limestone is the bedrock. The overlaying boulder clay has been washed down gaps and cracks which have formed in the limestone rock. These may then become sink holes and eventually something larger. They form in groups and look like a crater.

Ingleborough
2,375ft (724m)

Simon Fell 2,129ft (649m)

Chapel-le-Dale

Key Details (My Best Route)

Distance:	14.5km (9 miles)
Height to Climb:	560m (1,840ft)
O/S Explorer Map:	OL2 Yorkshire Dales South & West
Parking:	SD 746693. Clapham, Car Park.

My View

Ingleborough is many visitors' choice as 'favourite mountain in the Dales' and with good reason. The approaches to the mountain are excellent, each has a distinct character and is crowned by a satisfying summit plateau. The bedrock is limestone which, by its nature, brings two major advantages; not only are most of the paths relatively dry in most conditions, but the exposed rock gives a fresh, vibrant light adding significantly to the views. A shelter, two large cairns and a trig point adorn the summit of Ingleborough.

The walk up from Clapham is undeniably the best approach to Ingleborough and possibly the best route up any of the Dales 30. Woodland, Trow Gill, and Gaping Gill liven up the ascent, as does the pretty southern ridge leading to the summit plateau. The descent is also full of interest, mainly for the outstanding views towards the Forest of Bowland and the easy gradients. This is not a mountain to be climbed just once as there are a few other alternatives. Whilst Simon Fell is not easy from the Clapham ascent it is perfectly placed for an alternative approach from Ribblehead.

I have climbed Ingleborough many times as part of the Three Peaks Challenge and sections of the mountain are under considerable strain as a result of the number of walkers (particularly the climb from the Old Hill Inn). As of 2020 the entire upper section of the path (from the steep bit) to the summit has been repaired with considerable time and effort. It is now safer and easy to walk on.

Ingleborough

Ingleborough from near Simon Fell

Ingleborough

My Best Route *(from Clapham)*

1. Turn right from the car park in Clapham, cross the river and join the wide track (signposted to Ingleborough Cave). The initial walk is through pleasant woodland beside the lake of Clapdale before emerging from the trees after 1.5km. Ingleborough Cave is to the left (worth a visit; we once went as a family at Christmas and the cave was full of elves and Santa, excellent!) but the route carries on heading NNE. The path then turns sharply WNW into Trow Gill, a narrow cavern with a mini scramble at its head.

2. Emerging from Trow Gill the countryside opens up. After 200m there is a stile to the left, take it and head NW climbing towards Little Ingleborough. A short detour to the NE is worth taking to have a look at Gaping Gill. From the airy perch of Little Ingleborough a narrow grassy ridge heads north towards the summit plateau. The path emerges at the east end of the plateau 250m ESE of the summit cairn and shelter.

3. If only climbing Ingleborough, return to the cairn at the south east point of the flat plateau and follow the broad ridge back to Little Ingleborough. At this point leave the outbound path and follow the more intermittent path SSW. The descent is on easy slopes but the path is difficult to follow; don't worry as there is no steep ground hereabouts. The path turns very slowly south before emerging at a minor road at Newby Cote (2.5km from Little Ingleborough). Turn left at the road and return to Clapham.

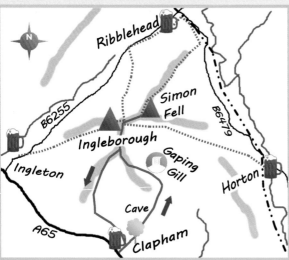

4. To include Simon Fell from the summit of Ingleborough, return east for 250m but to the northern end of the plateau where a large upright stone/ boulder reveals the start of a path. Drop steeply down to a stile and pick up a wall which leads due east to the summit of Simon Fell. Either return to the plateau of Ingleborough to pick up the route back to Clapham or, in good visibility, contour SW and join the ridge just to the north of Little Ingleborough.

Ingleborough

An Excellent Alternative *(from Ribblehead)*

1.   From the Station Inn at Ribblehead head SW on the road for 1.5km to 50m short of the Old Hill Inn. Cross a stile and follow a footpath south for nearly 2km past some wonderful limestone pavements.

2.   At a gate the nature of the walk changes. The next mile the track steepens over the wet moors. However, the path is dry; large boulders and duck boards have been air lifted in to improve this very busy path (part of the Three Peaks challenge). A short sharp climb zig zags to the main ridge. Turn WSW through a stile and follow the path to the summit plateau at its east end. It is a 250m walk to the summit cairn.

3.   From the plateau return to the gate at the top of the steep section. Follow a path ENE along the northern rim. After 300m head up hill to join a wall. Follow this to the summit of Simon Fell. From Simon Fell follow the wall north to a junction. This joins the path along the northern rim of Simon Fell and then up to the trig point of Park Fell. From here the path (to the left of the wall) drops steeply down NNE towards the farm at Colt Park. Turn north at the road and return to Ribblehead.

Gaping Gill

A natural cavern the size of York Minster opens up on the southern slopes of Ingleborough. It is possible to be winched in during May and August bank holidays (for a small charge) and is a truly memorable experience. Gaping Gill is just one of a number of large caverns and underground caves in this part of the Dales marking the area as having the best caving in England.

For a more leisurely exploration of these caves visit White Scar Caves to the north of Ingleborough.

A Popular Alternative *(from Ingleton)*

The direct route from Ingleton is probably the most popular way up and down Ingleborough (particularly for those who have limited navigation experience). The descent can be varied by heading north from the summit and exploring the wonderful limestone pavements above Raven Scar. It is trackless but a geologist's delight.

Typical Limestone Pavement

Whernside

Key Details (My Best Route)

Distance:	19.5km (12 miles)
Height to Climb:	610m (2,001ft)
O/S Explorer Map:	OL2 Yorkshire Dales South & West
Parking:	SD 704871 Dent, Car Park.

My View

When I first climbed Whernside (the highest mountain in Yorkshire) I found it highly enjoyable. We started from Dent and the ground was frozen all the way up to the summit. The large summit ridge (shaped like the keel of an upturned boat) makes for some fine walking with spectacular views all the way to the southern Lakes. On that winter's day the views were extensive, the underfoot terrain was excellent and the beer back at Dent highly enjoyable.

Most walkers complete the circuit of Whernside from Ribblehead. In itself the route is good, circling the wonderful Ribblehead viaduct on well constructed paths, but pick your day and time carefully. On any Saturday, during the summer months, thousands of boots will be tramping the paving stones of Whernside as the mid point and highest mountain is 'conquered' on the Three Peaks Challenge.

On these days those looking for the real Whernside need to head south of the summit ridge towards the limestone above Twisleton Scar or west towards lonely Gragareth and pretty Dentdale.

Many times, whilst guiding a group up Whernside, I have longed to hop over the summit wall and enjoy the peace that exists only yards from the crowds. Here you are unlikely to meet another soul, only the irregular barking of the red grouse breaking the silence of the moors.

Whernside & Ribblehead viaduct

Whernside

My Best Route

(from Dent)

1.   Join the Dales Way in Dent (turn east) and follow the river for 1.5km until it meets the road at a bridge over Deepdale Beck, just short of Whernside Manor. 50m beyond the bridge take a right fork in the road and then leave the tarmac and take the bridleway ESE after 50m. Here the path climbs steadily (initially zig zagging) for just over 2km before it starts to level off.

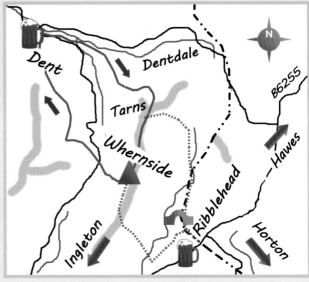

2.   Just past a wall to your right, at the high point of the track, a path heads south, staying close to the wall which remains to your right. Where the wall turns right carry on SSW until the land flattens and arrive at the three (or four) tarns of Whernside. Keep the tarns to the right and carry on up the path to another wall (coming in from the left) which is following the high shoulder of Whernside. It is a further 1km to the summit cairn and trig.

3.   From the summit head west, encountering a prominent cairn and then a wall half way down to Deepdale. On meeting the road turn north for 500m before taking to a walled lane on the left.

Force Gill

4. This is Occupation Road and adds an attractive alternative (in drier conditions) to the easy road descent back to Dent. The 'Road' contours the fellside for 6km with superb views of Dentdale throughout. After 6km with Dent directly below take the steep path down Flinter Gill into Dent.

Whernside

Approaching Whernside on the popular route

The Most Popular Route

(From Ribblehead) 7 miles

Take the track to Whernside from the road junction (where there is parking). Do not pass under the viaduct but continue to keep the railway on your left hand side. The track is flat as it passes Bleamore Sidings until it crosses the railway 1km further. Here there is a good view of the waterfall of Force Gill before the path climbs steeply NNW.

Cross a fence to the left after 1km and head NW then west. The path is excellent and unmissable as it climbs steadily to the shoulder of Whernside and then SSW to the summit.

Head SSW from the summit. After 1km the path turns SSE and drops steeply down the hillside. This section, still steep, has been recently repaired and is much more stable. Pass two stiles until the farm at Brunscar is met. After the outbuildings turn NE along a faint path until it meets the road to Gunnerfleet Farm (outdoor centre) and then cross under the viaduct and back to the start.

Highest in Yorkshire?

Anyone on the summit of Whernside is at the highest place in Yorkshire. Mickle Fell (20 miles further north) is the highest mountain in the historic county of Yorkshire at 788m but is now in County Durham.

Whernside is definitely the highest of the Dales 30!

Ribblehead

Work started in 1869 on the viaduct and the 2km tunnel under Blea Moor. There were nine Shanty towns that grew up with thousands of temporary workers. Oddly the nearest Shanty village was called Sebastopol and was the inspiration for the TV series Jericho (not filmed locally), but Jericho was in fact a different town a few miles away.

There are mounds of earth clearly visible beyond Blea moor Siding where the rock was dug and manufactured. There is also a ditch near the viaduct which is the old locomotive shed for the steam trains which moved the rock.

The other main remnant of the shanty towns are the 100 graves at Chapel le Dale (including children) who died in the smallpox that infected the camps.

Great Coum 2,254ft (687m)

Gragareth 2,060ft (628m)

Key Details (My Best Route)

Distance: 13km (8 miles)

Height to Climb: 490m (1,610ft)

O/S Explorer Map: OL2 Yorkshire Dales South & West

Parking: SD 671788 0.5km south of Leck Fell House, Road Side.

Near Leck House

My View

I had climbed Great Coum from Dent a few years prior to the much bigger day from Ireby. It was not satisfying, partly because the cloud was down, but mainly because I wanted to follow the full ridge including Gragareth. I was also keen to explore the rarely visited (except by archaeologists) Leck Valley of which I had heard good reports.

I took the advice of Wainwright (why wouldn't I), parked up in the small hamlet at Ireby (653754) and headed off. A bit of thought (and forgetting Wainwright would have been on foot) would have saved me a good two hours and 8km of walking as there is some parking available near Leck Fell House (described in the Best Route). Not to worry, it was a fine summer's day and I had plenty of time. It also offered me the opportunity to walk down the entire Leck Valley which proved to be an excellent decision. The shorter route from Leck Fell House does not offer that opportunity.

In the past I have always enjoyed striding out over the long grassy ridges of the eastern Lakes and the western Dales so the 4.5km from Gragareth, past Green Hill to Great Coum, proved to be a delightful hour or so. To the SW Crag Hill and its trig provides a memorable viewpoint and signifies the end of the grassy ridge. However, the walk is barely half complete with the joys of Leck Beck to follow. I ended up being out over five hours but was it worth it? Yes, it was.

Gragareth looking towards Great Coum

Great Coum

My Best Route *(from Leck Fell House, near Ireby)*

1.   To reach the start take the quiet fell road from Leck village for nearly 3km. There is some limited parking 500m short of Leck Fell House where a wall meets the road from the NE. Walk through the farm then double back and head steeply SE to the prominent three cairns of Gragareth. From the cairns turn east and on gradual, trackless slopes climb to the summit of Gragareth.

2.   A wall heads NNE and then north for 4km from Gragareth to Great Coum via Green Hill. It can be marshy in places, but wasn't when I was there. From Great Coum turn west and follow the wall to the trig point of Crag Hill, a fine viewpoint.

3.   Head SW, initially following the wall (becomes a fence) but where it turns WSW carry straight on. An indistinct path heads to a second wall, follow this SW towards Bullpot Farm. However, at 675818 cross the wall and take another path heading due south. At Ease Gill enjoy the odd rock formation and a disappearing river, classic limestone features. Follow the river bed WSW for nearly 1km before taking to the steep southern slopes of the beck.

4. Climb the steep slopes to a gate in a fence. Pass through the gate and take a faint path south over open fellside till meeting a field wall. Keep to the path next to the wall and head SE for 1km to the road and your start point.

5. To extend the walk start from Ireby (extra 8km). Head NNW for 500m from Ireby and carry on a farm lane for 2km until it meets the road to Leck House. On the return turn SW as you pass through the gate (in 4 above) and then SSW. Initially the path keeps high above Leck Gill but a path soon heads down to the gill and a pleasant walk back through woodland to Leck and then along the road to Ireby.

Crag Hill

The 'Dry' Valley

Birds of the Dales

Over 30 different species of birds can be spotted on any trip up the mountains of the Dales 30.

Most common are the flocks of smaller birds such as the curlews, snipe, lapwing and skylark whilst a cuckoo or a woodpecker is often heard but rarely seen.

Particularly memorable for residents of the Yorkshire Dales are the flocks of starlings which take to the air during the autumn months. They arrive en mass and provide a wonderful spectacle as they swoop and dive in a spectacular group display.

The most famous birds though are the peregrine falcons at Malham Cove. As well as mating for life they are the fastest species in the animal kingdom. They have been nesting at Malham since 1993 and are best seen between the end of March and early June. There are other nesting sites, as many as 20, across the area.

Another reasonably common bird of prey is the heron, much loved (amongst other places) in my own village of Long Preston where its graceful style is often seen beside the local beck.

Buzzards are the other birds of prey that you might spot in the skies.

Alternative Routes

(From Dent)

Great Coum is straightforward to climb from Dent. Take the path SSW for 1.25km until it meets a bridleway. Turn SE and follow this Green Lane for 1.5km (707848). At a wall take to the open fellside. Initially climb SW up steep slopes, the wall turns SSE and the ground eases. Follow the wall to the summit of Great Coum.

Having gone to Crag Hill I returned the same way. Gragareth is a long and inconvenient detour.

(From the East)

The quickest access to both summits is from the road at 723822 where a bridleway heads west past High Pike to within 100m of the summit ridge, midway between Great Coum and Gragareth.

Gragareth

The highest point in Lancashire, Gragareth lies 200m west of the boundary with Yorkshire.

Calf Top

Key Details (My Best Route)

Distance:	17km (10.5 miles)
Height to Climb:	590m (1,935ft)
O/S Explorer Map:	OL2 Yorkshire Dales South & West
Parking:	SD 628825 Barbon, Off Road.

Barbon Beck

My View

Amazing what a couple of centimetres does. In 2016 surveyors upgraded Calf Top so it broaches the magic 2,000 feet height and becomes a bona fida member of the Dales 30 (making it 30!). Excellent news as the ridge to the north of Barbondale offers some of the most pleasant walking in the neighbourhood, the dale itself being one of my favourites. A good excuse to re-visit.

Barbon is an attractive, out of the way village with a pub. It is famous (amongst those in the know) as the venue for the Barbon Hillclimb Championship. Run twice a year along the driveway of Barbon Manor the race is less than 1km long. However, I have never seen the race and it is the valley that bears the village name which I really enjoy. Barbondale is a classic U shaped valley (there is none better) with a pretty river winding gracefully down the floor of the dale. In the summer this is ideal for families splashing in the river and enjoying the scenery.

Up above, Calf Top is the highest point of the long ridge which flanks the dale. It is steep sided and uniform, contrasting with the more gradual lands to its north. The walking along the ridge is a delight with the short grass offering a better than even chance of surviving without damp feet. The main route finding decision is whether to take the direct descent from the summit or the more leisurely, but longer, descent beyond Calf Top, the latter is my recommendation.

Calf Top from the Lune Valley

Calf Top

My Best Route *(from Barbon)*

Barbondale

1. From the Barbon Inn cross the river just east of the church, the start of the driveway of Barbon Manor. Leave the road due north after 200m and head across to the corner of a wooded copse. Walk to the east of the woods for 500m to Eskholme House. Turn due east and join a faint footpath heading uphill. The path becomes more obvious and climbs steadily to a large well-constructed cairn at 307m with great views. Keep climbing for a further 1.8km turning NE then north. This is Castle Knott.

2. From here to the summit the walk is a delight with 1.8km of good views; to the north is the Howgills and southern Lakes, while to the east Gragareth blocks much but not all of the Three Peaks.

From the summit cairn it is possible to reverse your route by 100m and drop steeply down into Barbondale, but the walk is enhanced by carrying on along the ridge for 1.5km to Combe Top, past it and dropping down ENE over less steep slopes.

3.   The slopes lead to a footpath lower down and eventually the road just on the wrong side of the col. From here it is a 4km walk either along the road or along the pleasant verges, it is open walking and, away from hot summer days, very quiet. I always find it a pleasure.

4.   At Barkin Bridge a bridleway crosses the river and heads west into the woods. The final 2.5km, heading west through the woods, affords a brief glimpse of the manor. By this stage the pub is probably a more appealing thought.

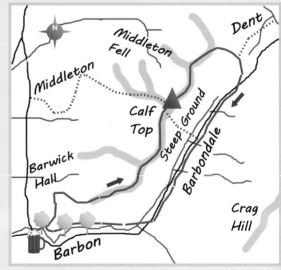

Calf Top

Calf Top summit trig

Alternative Routes

(Gawthrop in Dentdale)

A track skirts the fellside of Combe Scar to the NW of Gawthrop which meets the slopes of the Best Route descent. From here climb steadily to Combe Top and SW to Calf Top.

There is little option but to retrace your steps on the return.

(Middleton to the west)

The quickest option is to make use of the landrover tracks to the south of Middleton which heads east up part of the fellside.

Then a trackless climb leads to the summit.

The Longest network of caves

Stretching for over 41 miles the network of caves accessed from Barbondale and running under Leck, Ireby and Casterton Fells is said to be the longest and most complex in the country.

Known as the Ease Gill system much of the challenge is underwater.

Surveying our Mountain Tops

In 2010 three surveyors spent six hours, over two days taking accurate GPS readings of Calf Top using professional and expensive equipment. They sent the data to the Ordnance Survey for analysis and were gutted to find that the height was still 2cm or nearly an inch under the 2,000ft mark. 2000ft is significant as it denotes a mountain using unofficial British criteria.

All heights are based upon Ordnance Survey base stations whose own height is extremely accurate and a geoid model used to ascertain the height from this station.

Amazingly in 2016 a new geoid system produced even greater accuracy than previously and resulted in a 2cm to 4cm difference from the original survey on Calf Top.

Insignificant for pretty much every hill in Britain (the Scottish increase was more than 4cm) it was very significant for Calf Top as it raised the height to 609.58m or 2,000ft. Calf Top had become a mountain.

As an aside, what may also be an, as yet not discussed, consequence of global warming is a higher official sea (base) level. Imagine every mountain height being reduced by one metre? Food for thought!

Three Peaks Challenge

Heather Thomas Smith is an experienced guide who regularly takes large groups over the Three Peaks (and elsewhere). She has some interesting views on this world famous challenge...

Summit of Pen-y-Ghent

When asked how long I have been guiding walks and, especially, the Yorkshire Three Peaks I have to pause and think a little. There was a time when one didn't necessarily have to be a Mountain Leader; you just needed the right grounding. Having trained and served in the Mountain Rescue in Scotland in the early eighties my experience was considered sufficient to run the university's Fell Walking Club. After organising and leading various trips to Wales and the Lake District I led my first Yorkshire Three Peaks in the autumn of 1987.

Arriving late one Friday night with a bunch of likeminded students we had camped at Holme Farm in Horton in Ribblesdale. Next morning, full of the vigour, energy and 'go get 'em' attitude that we often have at that age, we had set off at full tilt, clockwise, to avoid meeting too many other folk. It was surprisingly peaceful. But our group was mismatched for speed. Leading the faster group down Whernside (a steep direct descent that is no longer used) I soon realised that the latter part of the group were get-

ting too far behind. We even had time for a pint at the Station Inn. By the time my second had caught up it was evident that we were not going to make the full round as one group. Some were too tired, some had blisters. It was decision time. And the outcome may surprise.

The group voted that if we could not complete it, together, then we would walk back to Horton in the gathering dusk and ascend Pen-y-Ghent, together, the next morning. The Sunday weather was foul but despite that and the fact the Three Peaks had now been attained over two days all were happy they had given it a go. We were young and there would be another time. Everyone had already walked further in one day than they had ever done, an achievement in itself.

I did not return for several years and when I did so it was pandemonium. The fells were overrun by a seemingly endless large-scale event and we had to queue with our dog to get up Whernside.

The footpath erosion was worse than ever – although it had long been a problem - and there was rubbish everywhere. I vowed never to return. I researched challenge and charity events (especially The National and Yorkshire Three Peaks) and their effect on the environment, local communities and Mountain Rescue teams. I wrote articles. I was dismayed at the effect these events were having despite their good causes and wished to see a better way forward; I called it 'Balancing the Challenge'.

In 2000 I moved to the Dales and was regularly walking over one or more of the Three Peaks, but not on a Saturday unless starting from the Hill Inn or Ribblehead. I had learnt to enjoy the peace of the hills. I had to change my game. I collected rubbish on Whernside and studied the area and its fabulous history and geology. My visits usually involved different routes, different challenges. Then I qualified as a Mountain Leader so I could lead walks for GGUK.

Approaching Ingleborough

Job offers to lead the Three Peaks came in. Initially I declined thinking of the horror and effect of the masses I had encountered. I wanted to guide anywhere but the Three Peaks. However, there was another issue to consider. If people were fired up to do the Three Peaks they were going to undertake the challenge anyway. Maybe I could give them the opportunity to see a little more, to enjoy the beautiful Dales' landscape, its geology and history,

to learn how to be responsible in our fragile environment and to achieve something - usually for charity - they may never do without a guide. And so my guiding of the Three Peaks began.

Over the last few years I have thoroughly enjoyed leading countless groups through all kinds of conditions; many have faced numerous challenges depending on weather and their fitness, health, general outdoor knowledge, kit, background and language. Not everyone manages all three peaks, but each and every peak is an achievement.

The Challenge is demanding and it is about being prepared – those that don't bother often fail or do not gain from it - whether it be through attaining the right level of fitness, having a positive attitude, wearing the right shoes or bringing the required gear.

Addleborough

1,580ft (481m) A good little-un

Addleborough

*T*he simple reason that Addleborough is one of the more popular hills in the Dales is that it looks good! The flat shaped summit (a mini Matterhorn, certainly a mini Ingleborough) draws the eye when driving or walking in Wensleydale and demands further exploration. It is not large, a mere 1,580ft, but the approaches are straightforward and the summit area full of interest. It is thought that the Ancient Britons had a burial site on the highest point, marked by a still visible cup and ring display of stones, whilst the Romans used the plateau as a key look out point.

Best Route 9.5km (6 miles): Starting at the small village of Thornton Rust a bridleway heads SW for 1.5km to a gate where an obvious track (not marked on the map) heads north steeply to the summit plateau. The highest point is to the north of the plateau. The descent from here is tricky. I headed east away from the ring of small cliffs for roughly 200m and then headed down steep slopes to meet a bridleway to the north. From here the path heads NE back to Cubeck and along a lane to Thornton Rust.

Kisdon Fell

1,638ft (499m) A good little-un

In the centre of large expanses of moorland masquerading as mountains lies pretty Kisdon Fell. It occupies a small area in Upper Swaledale, cut off by the deep divide of the River Swale, and surrounded by three lovely and pleasantly unspoilt Dales villages. The summit area is little more than 1km by 0.5km and is surrounded by steep sides in all directions; whether climbing from Keld, Thwaite or Muker it is an effort.

Best Route 12km (7.5 miles): I climbed Kisdon Fell from Thwaite (Muker is just as good) on my first visit, steeply crossing the fellside to the southern end of the broad ridge. Having climbed to the summit I returned to the bridleway and descended NNW into Keld. From Keld I followed the River Swale back to Muker and thereafter Thwaite, a delightful circuit and one of the best walks in the Dales. Near Muker there are some wonderful hay meadows (preserved fields full of wild flowers) and a walk through these in June will only enhance an already good walk.

Stone barn on Kisdon Fell

Aye Gill Pike

1,824ft (556m) A good little-un

From near Gawthrop

I have included Aye Gill Pike for a number of reasons. The hill overlooks Dentdale (and is in many ways Dent's hill) and therefore a good reason to visit this unfrequented dale. In addition, the hill itself is graceful and cuts an elegant profile (just look on a map to see this). Shaped like the hull of an over turned boat the views are also excellent. If a hill stood in the centre of the Dales 30 then Aye Gill Pike does this. The topography of the hills is laid out impressively from its broad shoulder. Finally the fell is rarely visited and frankly should be!

Best Route 9.5km (6 miles): From Dent head west along the river to Barth Bridge and start the climb from here. The ascent takes you initially through some farms to a low point on the broad east/west shoulder of Aye Gill Pike. Cross a wall and then follow it gradually to the summit of the fell, a pleasant and not onerous climb. I descended directly towards Dent from 100m to the west of the trig point, it is steep but quick. Others have suggested carrying on east along the ridge all the way towards Cowgill but it makes for a long day.

Simon's Seat

1,591ft (485m) A good little-un

There are fewer higher fells to the south and east of the National Park but Simon's Seat is an exception. It and its neighbour Earl Seat (part of Bardon Fell) stand proud to the east of the River Wharfe and north of the popular beauty spot near Bolton Abbey. Legend has it the name Simon's Seat comes from Simon Magus who was followed by druids who thought he was one of the three Wise Men!

Best Route 13km (8 miles): Most people approach from near Cavendish Pavilion, just north of Bolton Abbey. It is the best approach to the mountain. It is also clearly signed on good paths. The walk starts through the splendidly named Valley of Desolation before the nature of the walk changes above some woodland and through a gate. Open fellsides of heather, bracken and tumbledown granite outcrops characterise the walk from here to the summit of Simon's Seat. It is worthwhile exploring the area near the summit before returning south back to a nice cuppa and cake at the cafe. One word of warning, at present the estate does not allow dogs on the fell which is a shame.

From Appletreewick

Dales 30 Listing

<table>
<tr><th colspan="7">Dales 30 by Height</th></tr>
<tr><th></th><th>Walk</th><th>Area</th><th>Height (ft)</th><th>Height (m)</th><th>1/25,000 Map Ref.</th><th>High Point</th></tr>
<tr><td>1</td><td>Whernside</td><td>Western Dales</td><td>2,415</td><td>736</td><td>OL2</td><td>SD 739 814</td></tr>
<tr><td>2</td><td>Ingleborough</td><td>Western Dales</td><td>2,375</td><td>724</td><td>OL 2</td><td>SD 741 746</td></tr>
<tr><td>3</td><td>Great Shunner Fell</td><td>Northern Dales</td><td>2,349</td><td>716</td><td>OL 30</td><td>SD 849 973</td></tr>
<tr><td>4</td><td>High Seat</td><td>Cumbrian Pennines</td><td>2,326</td><td>709</td><td>OL19</td><td>NY 802 013</td></tr>
<tr><td>5</td><td>Wild Boar Fell</td><td>Cumbrian Pennines</td><td>2,323</td><td>708</td><td>OL19</td><td>SD 758 988</td></tr>
<tr><td>6</td><td>Great Whernside</td><td>Upper Wharfedale</td><td>2,310</td><td>704</td><td>OL 2</td><td>SE 002 739</td></tr>
<tr><td>7</td><td>Buckden Pike</td><td>Upper Wharfedale</td><td>2,303</td><td>702</td><td>OL 30</td><td>SD 961 788</td></tr>
<tr><td>8</td><td>Pen-y-Ghent</td><td>Western Dales</td><td>2,277</td><td>694</td><td>OL 2</td><td>SD 838 734</td></tr>
<tr><td>9</td><td>Great Coum</td><td>Western Dales</td><td>2,254</td><td>687</td><td>OL 2</td><td>SD 701 836</td></tr>
<tr><td>10</td><td>Swarth Fell</td><td>Cumbrian Pennines</td><td>2,234</td><td>681</td><td>OL19</td><td>SD 755 967</td></tr>
<tr><td>11</td><td>Plover Fell</td><td>Western Dales</td><td>2,231</td><td>680</td><td>OL 2</td><td>SD 848 753</td></tr>
<tr><td>12</td><td>Baugh Fell, Tarn Rigg</td><td>Cumbrian Pennines</td><td>2,224</td><td>678</td><td>OL19</td><td>SD 740 916</td></tr>
<tr><td>13</td><td>The Calf</td><td>The Howgills</td><td>2,218</td><td>676</td><td>OL19</td><td>SD 667 971</td></tr>
<tr><td>14</td><td>Lovely Seat</td><td>Northern Dales</td><td>2,214</td><td>675</td><td>OL 30</td><td>SD 879 951</td></tr>
<tr><td>15</td><td>Calders</td><td>The Howgills</td><td>2,216</td><td>675</td><td>OL19</td><td>SD 671 961</td></tr>
<tr><td>16</td><td>Great Knoutberry Hill</td><td>Northern Dales</td><td>2,205</td><td>672</td><td>OL 2</td><td>SD 789 872</td></tr>
<tr><td>17</td><td>Rogan's Seat</td><td>Northern Dales</td><td>2,205</td><td>672</td><td>OL 30</td><td>NY 920 031</td></tr>
<tr><td>18</td><td>Dodd Fell Hill</td><td>Northern Dales</td><td>2,192</td><td>668</td><td>OL 30</td><td>SD 841 846</td></tr>
<tr><td>19</td><td>Fountains Fell</td><td>Western Dales</td><td>2,192</td><td>668</td><td>OL 30</td><td>SD 864 716</td></tr>
<tr><td>20</td><td>Little Fell</td><td>Cumbrian Pennines</td><td>2,188</td><td>667</td><td>OL19</td><td>SD 808 971</td></tr>
<tr><td>21</td><td>Simon Fell, Ingleborough</td><td>Western Dales</td><td>2,129</td><td>649</td><td>OL 2</td><td>SD 754 751</td></tr>
<tr><td>22</td><td>Yockenthwaite Moor</td><td>Upper Wharfedale</td><td>2,110</td><td>643</td><td>OL 30</td><td>SD 909 811</td></tr>
<tr><td>23</td><td>Fell Head</td><td>The Howgills</td><td>2,099</td><td>640</td><td>OL19</td><td>SD 649 982</td></tr>
<tr><td>24</td><td>Yarlside</td><td>The Howgills</td><td>2,096</td><td>639</td><td>OL19</td><td>SD 686 985</td></tr>
<tr><td>25</td><td>Gragareth</td><td>Western Dales</td><td>2,060</td><td>628</td><td>OL 2</td><td>SD 688 793</td></tr>
<tr><td>26</td><td>Darnbrook Fell</td><td>Western Dales</td><td>2,047</td><td>624</td><td>OL 30</td><td>SD 885 728</td></tr>
<tr><td>27</td><td>Randygill Top</td><td>The Howgills</td><td>2,047</td><td>624</td><td>OL19</td><td>NY 687 001</td></tr>
<tr><td>28</td><td>Drumaldrace, Wether Fell</td><td>Northern Dales</td><td>2,014</td><td>614</td><td>OL 30</td><td>SD 874 867</td></tr>
<tr><td>29</td><td>Birks Fell</td><td>Upper Wharfedale</td><td>2,003</td><td>610</td><td>OL 30</td><td>SD 919 764</td></tr>
<tr><td>30</td><td>Calf Top</td><td>Western Dales</td><td>2,000</td><td>610</td><td>OL 2</td><td>SD 664 857</td></tr>
</table>

Dales 30 Log of Climbs

Log of Climbs			
Date Climbed	**Companions**	**Weather**	**Other Details**

About the Author

Jonathan has lived and walked in the Dales for over 20 years. He is a qualified Mountain Leader with many years guiding under his belt including repeated circuits on the Yorkshire Three Peaks. In 2010 he turned his passion into a career and set up Where2walk with the aim of making it the 'come to' website for anyone wanting to walk in the north of Britain.

The Where2walk website now describes over 500 individual walks, several long distance trails and a number of walking challenges including the 'Dales 30'. Jonathan runs navigation courses in the Dales, offers a guiding service and sells bespoke walking holidays for those wanting to taste the pleasures of walking in our upland areas.

Jonathan has completed the Munros (and Tops), the Wainwrights (twice) and will take any detour (long or short) to get to the highest point in the area. It is rare to see him without his loyal border collie, Mist.

The Dales 30 is Jonathan's first book. Two years later he released a second, "The Yorkshire 3 Peaks", an illustrated guide to the history of this famous walking challenge in the Yorkshire Dales.